CYCLING IN
THE LAKE DISTRICT

About the Author

After years of road running and mountaineering had wreaked havoc with his knees, Richard Barrett returned to long-distance cycling in his 50s when he bought himself a classic British-made touring bike. Now in his 60s, he rides a handmade bike from one of the great British frame makers that have appeared in recent years. Combined with sea-kayaking, cycling allows him to continue his love affair with the more mountainous parts of the UK which he first visited as a teenager.

His career was spent in marketing in a number of multinational organisations in the UK and abroad, but he now lives on North Harris in the Western Isles where he and his wife enjoy an active and busy retirement.

Other Cicerone guides by the author
Cycling in the Hebrides
Walking on Harris and Lewis

CYCLING IN
THE LAKE DISTRICT

by Richard Barrett

2 POLICE SQUARE, MILNTHORPE, CUMBRIA LA7 7PY
www.cicerone.co.uk

© Richard Barrett 2016
First edition 2016
ISBN-13: 978 1 85284 778 4

Printed by KHL Printing, Singapore
A catalogue record for this book is available from the British Library.

Route mapping by Lovell Johns www.lovelljohns.com
All photographs are by the author unless otherwise stated.
© Crown copyright 2016 OS PU100012932.
NASA relief data courtesy of ESRI

Acknowledgements

My thanks to everyone who accompanied me on these rides; those I spent just a few miles with before we parted company and the chums of a quarter of a century who still meet every May for a week of hostel touring and fine dining: Nick Cloke, Simon Wheeler and latterly, my nephew, Ashley Broad. They appear in many of the photographs as do our family friends, Paul Rigby and his son James, who joined me on a few of the rides. Mention should also be made of all the helpful staff and volunteers at the many hostels I used during my rides. I also need to thank Jonathan Williams of Cicerone for his ready acceptance of my proposal and Stephanie, Lois, Caroline and the rest of the team, who once again made the production process such a pleasure – and lastly my partner Cindy for her diligent proof reading.

Updates to this Guide

While every effort is made by our authors to ensure the accuracy of guidebooks as they go to print, changes can occur during the lifetime of an edition. Any updates that we know of for this guide will be on the Cicerone website (www.cicerone.co.uk/778/updates), so please check before planning your trip. We also advise that you check information about such things as transport, accommodation and shops locally. Even rights of way can be altered over time. We are always grateful for information about any discrepancies between a guidebook and the facts on the ground, sent by email to info@cicerone.co.uk or by post to Cicerone, 2 Police Square, Milnthorpe LA7 7PY, United Kingdom.

Front cover: Riding down the zig-zags at Martindale with Howtown below (Route 5)

CONTENTS

Route symbols on map extracts

~~ route
~~ variant
~~ route takes ferry
~~ railway line
⟩ route direction
🚲 start point
🚲 finish point
🚲 start/finish point
🏠 hostel
⌂ camping barn

Route map scale 1:200,000 (1cm = 2km)
(except 1:100,000 maps in Stage 2A and Route 2)

Features on the overview map

Area of Outstanding Natural Beauty, eg *Solway Coast*

~~ Railway line

800m +
600m
400m
200m
75m
0m

GPX files

GPX files for all routes can be downloaded for free at www.cicerone.co.uk/778/GPX.

Descending Wrynose Pass (Route 1)

A TOUR OF THE LAKE DISTRICT

Stage	Start	via	Finish	Grade (discounting distance)	Distance km (miles)	Ascent (m)	Time (hr)	Page
1A	Ambleside	Kirkstone Pass	Troutbeck	Challenging	35 (21)	750	4–5	55
1B	Ambleside	Shap	Troutbeck	Moderate	75 (46)	1111	8–9	60
2A	Troutbeck	Threlkeld	Keswick	Easy	14 (9)	76	1	67
2B	Troutbeck	Hesket Newmarket	Keswick	Hard	46 (29)	620	4–5	71
3A	Keswick	Honister, Newlands, Whinlatter,	Cockermouth	Challenging	51 (32)	1085	6–7	77
3B	Keswick	Lorton	Cockermouth	Hard	44 (28)	794	5–6	83
4A	Cockermouth	Ennerdale, Wasdale	Eskdale Green	Hard	56 (35)	897	6–7	88
4B	Cockermouth	Egremont, Wasdale	Eskdale Green	Moderate	65 (41)	792	6–7	96
5A	Eskdale Green	Hardknott, Wrynose	Ambleside	Challenging	35 (22)	830	5–6	103
5B	Eskdale Green	Coniston	Ambleside	Hard	57 (36)	1450	7–8	107

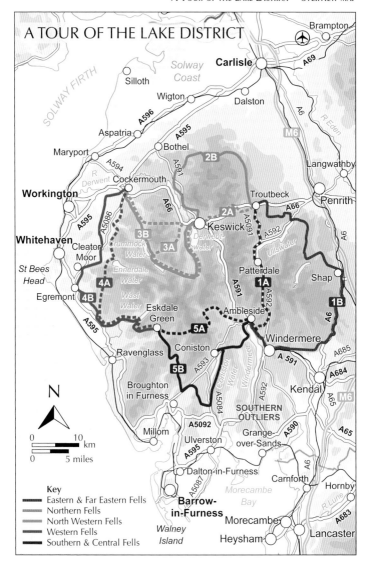

A TOUR OF THE LAKE DISTRICT

Brampton

Carlisle

Solway Coast

Silloth

Wigton

Dalston

SOLWAY FIRTH

Aspatria

Bothel

2B

Maryport

Cockermouth

Langwathby

Workington

Troutbeck

Penrith

Keswick

2A

Whitehaven

Cleator Moor

3B

Derwent-water

St Bees Head

3A

Crummock Water

Patterdale

1A

Shap

Ullswater

Ennerdale Water

Egremont

4A

4B

Wast Water

Eskdale Green

Ambleside

1B

5A

Windermere

Ravenglass

Coniston

5B

Broughton in Furness

Kendal

SOUTHERN OUTLIERS

N

0   10 km

0   5 miles

Millom

Ulverston

Grange-over-Sands

Dalton-in-Furness

Carnforth

Hornby

Key

━━━ Eastern & Far Eastern Fells
━━━ Northern Fells
━━━ North Western Fells
━━━ Western Fells
━━━ Southern & Central Fells

Barrow-in-Furness

Morecambe Bay

Walney Island

Morecambe

Heysham

Lancaster

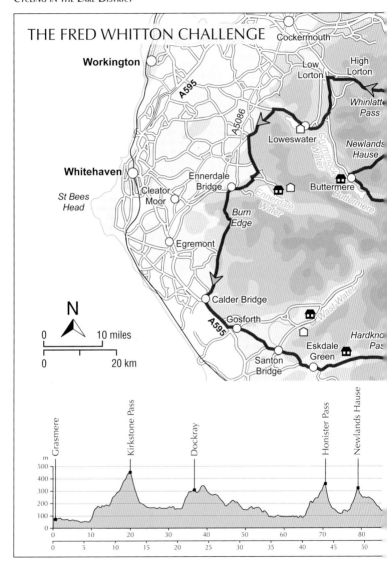

THE FRED WHITTON CHALLENGE

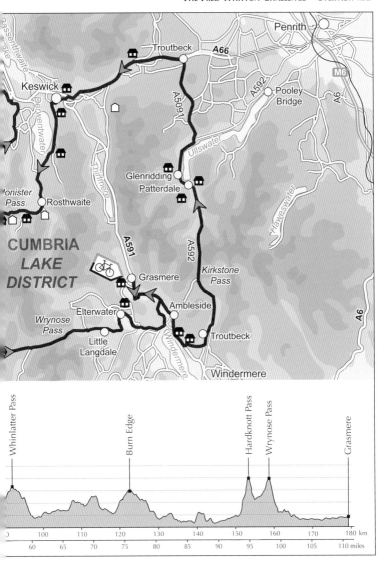

DAY RIDES

No	Start/Finish	Title	Grade (discounting distance)	Distance km (miles)	Ascent (m)	Time (hr)	Page
1	Ambleside	Wrynose and Hardknott passes	Challenging	68 (42)	1580	6–7	112
2	Ambleside	Around the Central Fells	Moderate	31 (19)	506	2–3	119
3	Ambleside	Circuit of the Eastern Fells	Hard	66 (41)	1346	5–6	123
4	Shap	Haweswater and Ullswater	Hard	68 (42)	888	5–6	130
5	Penrith	Lowther Park and Ullswater	Moderate	57 (36)	575	4–5	136
6	Stainton	Around Inglewood Forest	Moderate	56 (35)	555	3–4	143
7	Keswick	Loop around the Back o' Skiddaw	Moderate	54 (34)	815	4–5	147
8	Keswick	Whinlatter and Honister passes	Challenging	46 (29)	1025	4–5	152
9	Cockermouth	Across Allerdale	Hard	60 (37)	1006	5–6	157
10	Eskdale Green	Back o' Sellafield and Wasdale Head	Moderate	64 (40)	622	4–5	162
11	Ravenglass	Far South West Fells	Hard	56 (35)	1087	5–6	167
12	Broughton in Furness	Around the Furness Fells	Challenging	46 (29)	1024	4–5	173
13	Grizedale	Around Grizedale Forest	Moderate	32 (20)	654	2–3	178
14	Cartmel	Across Windermere from Cartmel	Moderate	54 (34)	881	4–5	183
15	Grange-over-Sands	A circuit around Whitbarrow	Hard	46 (29)	504	3–4	187

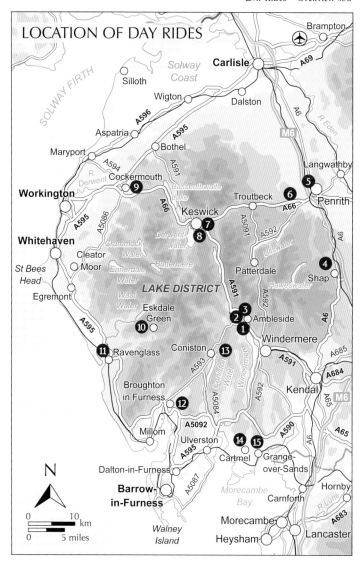

LOCATION OF DAY RIDES

Wasdale Screes in crisp spring sunshine (Stages 4A and 4B and Route 10)

INTRODUCTION

A heavily berried holly tree on the climb around Lingmoor Fell with the Langdale Pikes in the distance (Stage 5A and Route 2)

This compact and easily accessible corner of the North West is packed with the best of everything that England has to offer including cycling. It has all of the land over 914m (3000 feet) with England's highest summits, the largest and deepest lakes and rare wildlife such as red squirrels, nesting osprey and a solitary golden eagle that desperately needs a mate. The scenery was wild and dramatic before man arrived, first settling in the fertile valleys to grow crops and rear cattle, and then venturing into the fells to mine copper, lead and other ores. By medieval times the region was criss-crossed by packhorse tracks that linked the main commercial centres of Ambleside and Keswick with the outside world. Over time these tracks became the roads we know today. Some have very steep gradients and cross the highest passes in England providing cyclists with challenging rides amid stunning scenery.

Over the last 150 years, the growth of tourism and outdoor activities has transformed the region, particularly the eastern and central parts that are more easily accessible to those visiting for a weekend or just a day. Today, Ambleside, which a century ago was still a small market town, has accommodation and eateries to suit all pockets, outdoor shops in every direction and an increasing number of specialist retailers selling excellent locally produced foods. Then to mitigate the risk of tourists staying away during the colder, greyer months, there is an increasingly busy calendar of festivals in the region covering everything from beer and food to film and jazz. This means that the main towns of the district are now tourist destinations in their own right almost regardless of the fells and lakes that surround them, adding another layer of interest and variety to this beautiful part of the country.

There are numerous opportunities for easy, family-orientated cycling on traffic-free trails and quiet lanes around the shores of many lakes. But that's not what this guide is about. This book caters for those who want to tour through the mountains and valleys of England's largest national park, perhaps crossing one or more of the six famous passes which are all over 305m above sea level with gradients that occasionally touch 1 in 3 (33 per cent). While none of these climbs is high by European standards, the narrowness of the valleys in the Lake District means that roads have to take a direct route to the top rather than meandering their way up, resulting in sections with gradients that would be classified as *hors catégorie* in the Tour de France. Thankfully, they are just a fraction of the length of the classic climbs found in the Alps and the Pyrenees, but

they are challenging to ride so need a good level of fitness.

LAKE DISTRICT NATIONAL PARK

Until the region was popularised in William Wordsworth's (1770–1850) 1820 edition of *A guide through the District of the Lakes*, it would have been a relatively wild and inaccessible area seen as uncivilised and dangerous for travellers. Wordsworth was born in Cockermouth and educated at Hawkshead. In 1799 he settled in Grasmere living at Dove Cottage until his growing family forced him to move to Allan Bank in 1808, then the Old Rectory in 1810 and finally Rydal Mount in 1813. He lived there for the remainder of his life surrounded by a group of similarly Romantic writers and poets now known as the Lake Poets. Wordsworth described the district as 'a sort of national property, in which every man has a right and an interest who has an eye to perceive and a heart to enjoy'. But his enthusiasm for others to enjoy the landscape did not stop him protesting against the railway being extended to Windermere in 1847, perhaps with good reason as what had been a peaceful lakeside hamlet originally called Birthwaite became instantly accessible to the wealthy professionals and businessmen of the Northern cities and mill towns who quickly transformed the landscape by building lavish villas as weekend retreats. Hotels and boarding houses rapidly followed to accommodate the 120,000 tourists who visited the now fashionable resort every year during the second half of the 19th century. As tourism grew, the wealthy ventured further afield, building or acquiring grand country retreats, leaving the towns to holiday makers and day trippers.

By the early 20th century, mandatory holidays for workers and a growing appreciation of the outdoors led to demands for greater access to the countryside. This created conflict between landowners and public interest groups such as the Ramblers' Association, the Youth Hostels Association and the Council for the Preservation of Rural England who pressed the government for greater access. After World War II, the movement towards creating

national parks gained momentum resulting in the establishment of the Peak District National Park and Lake District National Park in 1951. Today there are 15 national parks in the UK with the Lake District being the largest, covering an area of 2292sq km (885sq miles) with plans afoot to increase it further.

Despite being called the Lake District, there is only one lake – Bassenthwaite Lake – everything else being 'waters', 'meres' or, in the case of the smaller expanses of water, 'tarns'. Some are not even natural. Thirlmere and Haweswater were created by damming natural valleys in the 1890s and 1930s to supply water for the towns and cities of Lancashire.

Similarly the picturesque Tarn Hows may look as though it has been

Daffodils at the gates of Dalemain House, near to where William Wordsworth saw the host of blooms that inspired his famous poem

FRANK PATTERSON – THE WAINWRIGHT OF THE ROADS

Rydal Water by Frank Patterson, reproduced with the kind permission of the CTC, the national cycling charity, www.ctc.org.uk

Many walkers hold the name of Alfred Wainwright (1907–1991) close to their hearts in that they will have used his *Pictorial Guide to the Lakeland Fells* to find their way to summits. However, few cyclists will have heard of the illustrator Frank Patterson (1871–1952), who provided over 26,000 drawings for *Cycling* magazine and then the *Cyclists' Touring Club Gazette* over a period of 59 years.

As a young man Patterson was an enthusiastic cyclist; this was curtailed by a leg injury when he was 38, and he then took up long distance walking. For the last 54 years of his life, he and his wife lived in a rented Elizabethan farmhouse near Billinghurst in Kent where he spent most of his time shooting on the land that he sub-let rather than farm. Leading a simple and contented life at home, he had little desire to travel and produced many of his later drawings from photographs and postcards sent by friends, dropping in a bike or some cyclists to satisfy his publisher. While his style is not to everyone's taste, his illustrations have a lasting appeal, both for their simple celebration of the British countryside – and for those traffic-free roads.

there forever, but it too is man-made. It was created in the mid-19th century for James Garth Marshall, MP and owner of nearby Monk Coniston Hall, as part of a series of landscaping projects he commissioned once he gained full possession of all the surrounding land after an enclosure act of 1862. In 1930 the Marshall family sold much of their land to Beatrix Heelis of Sawrey, – better known by her maiden name, the writer and illustrator Beatrix Potter – who then sold the half of this land containing the tarn to the National Trust and bequeathed the other half to them along with other land and properties in her will following her death in 1943.

Looking back it is fortuitous that the National Trust became such an important landowner and the Lake District National Park was established just at the right time. As the declining mining and quarrying were at risk of being replaced by other detrimental industries and as mass tourism was about to boom, these bodies came into being and were able to protect the landscape from unrestricted planning; some would say somewhat overzealously. But the attraction of the Lake District is its beauty and its easy accessibility and if it was not for its considered conservation by these two bodies it is doubtful whether so many of us would find it such a magnet.

GEOLOGY AND LANDSCAPE

The height of the Lake District fells has not much to do with the hardness of their rock, which is little different to that of the surrounding countryside, but to a raft of hard granite below, which occasionally breaks through at Eskdale, Ennerdale, Skiddaw and Shap. The top tier above this granite layer is made up of three broad bands of rock running from the southwest to the northeast.

In the north is the Skiddaw Group made up of the oldest rocks in the region formed through sedimentary action about 500 million years ago. Although they look like slate, they are friable and easily eroded, forming the rounded hills of the Northern Fells. South of this is the Borrowdale Volcanic Group made up of lavas and ash flows that erupted during a period of volcanic activity 450 million years ago. The highest and craggiest parts of the Lake District that are the most popular with walkers and climbers,

STONE WALLS

Rebuilding an old dry stone wall on the fell road above Staveley (Stage 1B)

Riding through the Lake District gives ample time to really get to know dry stone walls. Cumbria has an estimated 15,000km (9300 miles) of them, so there is a lot to study. Although some date from earlier times, most were constructed following the Enclosure Act of 1801 to divide up the farming landscape. The fields around farms in the valleys are known as in-bye fields, but the fields up the fellside have been 'taken' from the fell and are known as in-take fields. The land above the highest wall is the open fell.

Earlier walls tend to be built from well-rounded stones that retreating ice had left scattered across the landscape, whereas more recent walls were constructed from stone that was quarried in the immediate vicinity and dragged to where they were needed by a horse-drawn 'slipe' or sledge. This was not an easy task as each metre of wall requires a ton of stone.

Walls in the Lake District are built with a variety of different types of stone depending on the geology of the location with slate, shale, sandstone, limestone and granites all in common use. Traditionally craftsmen would build a 'rood' of wall a day; a measure that varied from seven yards (6.4 metres) down to six yards (5.48 metres) depending on how hard the local stone was to work with.

Lakeland walls generally have one or more layers of 'through-stones' laid across the wall to increase stability. Some have small rectangular 'smoots' at their base so hares and rabbits can pass from one field to the next. Others have larger holes in them variously known as sheep runs, cripple holes or sheep smoots to allow sheep to pass from one pasture to another.

such as Scafell (964m), Scafell Pike (978m), Helvellyn (950m), Coniston Old Man (803m) and the Langdale Pikes (736m), are all formed from the harder rocks of the Borrowdale Volcanic Group. Further south again is another zone of sedimentary slates, siltstones and sandstones known as the Windermere Group, which were formed during the Silurian period about 420 million years ago. Again being far less resistant to erosion, they form the rounded hills that stretch all the way from the Duddon estuary across to Kendal giving the southern part of the Lake District a more pastoral feel.

Some 400 million years ago the fells would have been of Himalayan proportions as violent volcanic activity pushed up from below to form a very high mountain range. But millions of years of erosion have reduced them to their present size, exposing igneous intrusions, which originally cooled and crystallised hundreds of metres below the surface. About 350 million years ago, most of the land sank beneath a warm tropical sea that teemed with life. The remains of these life forms created a thick layer of sediment made up of shells, fossils and coral all over the seabed, which eventually formed the pale grey Carboniferous limestone that runs around the perimeter of the national park. In other areas to the west, this sea was filled in with fertile mud and sand that resulted in the growth of forests, which decayed to form the belt of coal that was the lifeblood of heavy industry in West Cumbria.

During the last two million years, the Earth has gone through repeated

A monument in slate at the summit of Honister Pass (Stages 3A and 3B, and Route 8)

21

periods of glaciations separated by warmer periods that supported the growth of broadleaved forests. It is the action of glaciers and the continual freezing and thawing of melt water during this period that has shaped the fells we know so well today. After the last period of glaciation, the sea levels changed and soils formed below the oak forests in the valleys. However, clearing the forests for cultivation in the 11th century led to some soil erosion and the formation of alluvial fans and lake deltas characteristic of the central and southern parts of the region.

Since then, the only observable changes to the landscape have been due to the activity of man, either creating fields for livestock or mining and quarrying for minerals and building materials. Over the centuries, rock has been quarried for constructing buildings and the many miles of dry stone walls and slate for roofing. At the same time, lead, copper and other ores have been mined from veins in the rocks of the Borrowdale Volcanic Group at various sites in the centre of the area particularly during the 18th and 19th centuries. Today there is still some limited quarrying within the boundaries of the Lake District National Park, but by the 20th century mining had largely ended as financially viable veins of ore became exhausted.

The coastal region of West Cumbria has a particularly fascinating industrial history, revealed in local museums and heritage centres. Shipbuilding, coal and iron ore mining, steel making and chemical manufacturing have all been major employers, but today little of these industries remain.

PLANTS AND WILDLIFE

Cumbrian fell ponies still live wild in the Eastern Fells, ospreys nest in the woods above Bassenthwaite and a solitary golden eagle inhabits the hills around the head of Haweswater. However, you are unlikely to see them from your bike. Nevertheless, there is plenty of wildlife to see if you stay alert. The cavities in stone walls provide both shelter and hunting ground for the insect eating wren. Their constant movement makes them difficult to spot, but if you hear their trilling call, stop and you will catch sight of them bobbing about ahead of you. After the wood pigeon and the chaffinch, it is one of the commonest birds in the UK with an estimated population of seven to eight million; its success due to its ability to thrive in a varied range of habitats.

When riding along quieter lanes, you may occasionally find your presence has disturbed a large bird of prey from its perch and catch sight of it silently moving through the tree canopy above. Most likely, it is a common buzzard. Despite being much smaller than the golden eagle, it is still a formidable predator, dropping down on rabbits and small mammals, which

Primroses – one of the many wild flowers found along the verges in the Lake District

they nearly always kill on the ground. You may also see them hovering high in the sky and hear their plaintive mewing call, especially in spring when they are displaying to potential mates. In recent years, their numbers have exploded and they now thrive in areas where they were once a rarity.

When it comes to mammals, there is one very special species you should look out for – the red squirrel. Ever since Victorians released the North American grey squirrel into the wild in 1876, the red squirrel has been on the retreat. However, they still have a foothold in the woodlands in the northern parts of the Lake District and you may see one if you look for the road signs warning drivers of their presence. Contrary to popular belief, squirrels do not hibernate, as they need to eat all year round to survive, so look out for them right through the year. You may also see signs asking people to report sightings of any grey squirrels, which are increasing in numbers around the periphery of the national park. Conservation bodies are taking a number of steps to protect and promote the population of red squirrels. These include providing special feeders that only the reds can access and putting squirrel ladders across busy roads so they can safely move from one area of woodland to another. Beatrix Potter, creator of Squirrel Nutkin, would surely approve.

As well as protecting animals, the National Park Authority and other conservation organisations are also involved in protecting threatened habitats and plant species. This includes different types of grassland, upland heaths and mires, which are important habitats for the rare natterjack toad. Protected plant species include juniper, which exists in patches alongside the road between Little Langdale and Blea Tarn, and various lichens and mosses. In total, the Lake District is home to eight National Nature Reserves and over a thousand Sites of Special Scientific Interest as well as a number of other conservation areas.

HISTORY AND CULTURE

The history of any region is always determined by its natural resources and the Lake District is no different. At least 5000 years ago, communities settled in the valleys, erecting stone circles such as Castlerigg and venturing into the fells for material to shape into stone axes, which have since been found at archaeological sites all over Britain. The Celts, Romans, Angles and Vikings all settled across the district leaving evidence of their presence in Roman forts, Viking crosses and in place names with Nordic elements such as 'thwaite' meaning clearing and 'beck' meaning stream.

During the 15th and 16th centuries, many fortified tower houses and pele towers, such as Dacre Castle, were built as protection against the 'Border Reivers' who repeatedly made raids into what was known as the 'Debateable Lands' to rustle cattle, pillage and extort money. Once

A patchwork of stone walls and barns in the Duddon Valley (Stage 5B and Routes 11 and 12)

the borderline between England and Scotland was finally agreed in 1552 raiding diminished. Then when the thrones of Scotland and England were united in 1603, King James embarked on the 'Pacification of the Borders', rounding up the main reiver families and deporting many of them to Ireland. Religious communities also settled in the Lake District during the Middle Ages. Cartmel Priory survives intact as the village church, the abbey at Shap was largely dismantled after the Dissolution of the Monasteries in the middle of the 16th century and an earlier abbey at Dacre was destroyed by Vikings in the 10th century.

Today we value the Lake District for recreation and enjoyment and tourism is the mainstay of the local economy. But its natural resources meant it was once a hive of industry. There is evidence of mining and

BOBBIN MILLS

When the Lancashire textile industry was at its height in the 19th and early 20th centuries it had an insatiable need for bobbins for spinning and weaving and the vast majority were turned at one of the 65 mills scattered across the Lake District. The woods and copses in the valleys were coppiced to supply birch, ash and oak of the right diameter and the fast flowing streams provided power to drive the lathes until superseded by steam.

Today, the most famous is Stott Park Bobbin Mill near the southern tip of Windermere, which was set up by John Harrison, a local farmer, in 1835 and ran until it was abandoned in 1971 when the arrival of plastic bobbins finally put it out of business. Attracted by its remarkable state of preservation, English Heritage acquired the mill in 1991 and turned it into a working museum. But even at its peak, Stott Park was a minor producer employing only 25 men and boys and producing a mere 12 million bobbins a year. Low Briery Mill on the banks of the River Greta east of Keswick produced 40 million bobbins each year, while Howk Mill in Caldbeck, which employed nearly 60 people at its peak, is thought to have made even more.

The American Civil War interrupted the supply of cotton during the 1860s and the bobbin industry suffered as a result. It never fully recovered, having to compete against textile manufacturers turning their own bobbins on steam-powered lathes at their factories and an influx of cheaper imports from abroad. Many mills diversified into other wooden products from rungs for ladders to tool handles and even toggles for fastening duffle coats. Today little remains other than a few notable ruins, many of the old mills having been converted into pleasant beck-side cottages.

CRAFT BREWERIES WITHIN THE LAKE DISTRICT NATIONAL PARK

Even the smallest amount of alcohol during the day can go straight to the legs and make for a hellish afternoon in the saddle. But beer lovers cannot visit the Lake District without quaffing a few of the fine ales and lagers made by the wonderful little craft breweries scattered across the region. So collect a bottle or two to enjoy at the end of the day.

- Barngates Brewery in Ambleside uses water from the local beck.
- Bowness Bay Brewery names most of its beers after the boats on Windermere.
- The Coniston Brewing Company started up in 1995 in the 400 years old Black Bull Inn.
- Cumbrian Legendary Ales, now based at Hawkshead, started up at the Kirkstile Inn in Loweswater, which is now the brewery tap.
- Ennerdale Brewery is run from a farm and brews real ale using spring water from nearby Croasdale Fell.
- Hawkshead Brewery started in an old barn at Hawkshead in 2002 but rapidly outgrew it and moved to a new brewery based in Chadwick's Mill, the old wood turning mill in Staveley where they have since added a beer hall.
- Established by the then landlord of the local pub, the Hesket Newmarket Brewery is now a cooperative and so too is the pub, each having a cross shareholding in the other.
- The Keswick Brewing Company set up in 2006 occupies a site in Brewery Lane, thought to have been used by the oldest recorded brewer in the town.
- Strands Brewery based at the Strands Inn in Nether Wasdale has brewed an eye-wateringly strong 9.5 per cent barley wine.
- The Watermill Inn and Brewery at Ings, a couple of miles east of Windermere, is the smallest of the Lakeland breweries but still manages to offer up to 16 different beers.
- The Wild Boar Brewery is based at the eponymous Wild Boar Inn at Gilpin, just east of Windermere.
- Beers from the Winster Valley Brewery can be found at the brewery tap, The Brown Horse Inn in Winster and many other Lakeland pubs and restaurants.

quarrying from the 12th century, but the Romans clearly quarried materials for roads and buildings locally. Over the centuries, lead, copper, zinc, baryte, haematite, tungsten, graphite, fluorite, and coal have all been mined and quarried on a small scale within the boundaries of the national park; today slate mining continues at the top of the Honister and Kirkstone passes. Coal, iron ore and haematite were mined on a large scale at sites in West Cumbria in the 19th and early 20th centuries. To the east, granite and limestone are still quarried at Shap.

Good transportation was essential to move materials out of the area and canals and then railways encroached into the region on all sides. Today trains still run on some of the branch lines, which have been lovingly preserved as tourist attractions, while other lines have been transformed into traffic-free cycle paths that form part of the National Cycle Network.

Since the mid-Victorian era, tourism has grown until it dominates the local economy. In 2013, nearly 16 million visitors spent over £1 billion creating the equivalent of 15,500 full time jobs, which is approximately 40 per cent of the total population of the national park, a proportion which would be substantially higher if only those of working age were considered. In addition, tourists have provided a ready market for the myriad of artists, craft workers, artisan food producers and micro-brewers found in the district.

A selection of books offering more interesting facts and figures about the Lake District can be found in Appendix D.

GETTING THERE

Hardened touring cyclists from Northern England and Southern Scotland will probably be happy to add an extra day or two either end of their visit to the Lake District and make use of one or more of the National Cycle Networks – see www.sustrans.org.uk – that will take them from near their home right into the heart of the district. Others from further afield and those pressed for time will need to consider other options.

By road

If you are averse to sitting in slow moving traffic, it is probably best to plan your journey to avoid the main arteries into the district on Friday evenings and Saturdays during peak holiday months and national holiday weekends. If you are planning to tour, the next challenge might be to find long stay parking. You could park considerately at a location on the periphery of the region and start your ride there rather than parking in one of the busy centres where you will pay for the privilege. However, the current weekly charge for the Lake District's official car parks at Brockhole, Buttermere, Coniston, Grasmere, Hawkshead, Langdale, Ravenglass, Thirlmere, Ullswater and

Windermere works out at less than £5 per day. That's not bad value and you can pay by mobile phone – see www.lakedistrict.gov.uk for details.

By air

The nearest airports are Manchester, Liverpool, Leeds/Bradford, Newcastle, Prestwick, Glasgow and Edinburgh. But arriving at any one of these airports still leaves you a journey of 100 miles or more to the Lake District, necessitating hiring a car or using public transport. If you are planning to fly with your bike, you should contact your airline and make a reservation when you book your seat. They will charge you for carrying your bike and will ask that you follow their packing instructions. These typically include turning and locking the handlebars parallel with the frame, removing the pedals and front wheel and attaching them to the frame and deflating the tyres before placing the bike in a carrying bag or transit box. If you are planning to tour, you will also need to organise somewhere to store the transit material ready for collection on your return.

By rail

The West Coast mainline operated by Virgin Trains runs to the east of the Lake District, connecting Oxenholme, Penrith and Carlisle with London and Glasgow. They provide special bike storage areas with space for up to four bikes or two tandems, but you will need to book a reservation for your bike before you travel. The service is free and can be made at any booking office or by

A train crossing the 50 spans of the Kent Viaduct

RAVENGLASS AND ESKDALE STEAM RAILWAY

If you are an enthusiast of steam trains, you might enjoy breaking your ride for an excursion out to the coast on the Ravenglass and Eskdale Steam Railway. There is space for four to six bikes on each train but boarding is only possible at Ravenglass and Dalegarth stations and wheelchair users receive priority. Tickets can be purchased online but must be presented at Ravenglass or Dalegarth ticket offices on arrival where they are exchanged for travel tickets. You also need to call Tel 01229 717171 to book cycles on to the train before boarding. See http:// ravenglass-railway.co.uk.

One of the 15in gauge locomotives on the Ravenglass and Eskdale Steam Railway (Routes 10 and 11)

calling Tel 0344 556 5650. On the day of travel, you will need to collect your bike reservation coupons at a FastTicket machine at the station, by keying in your FastTicket reference number and the number of the bank card you used to make the booking. Then give yourself a minimum of 10 minutes to contact a member of the Virgin platform staff who will help you load your bicycle. Once aboard, inform the Train Manager that you have a bicycle and he or she will help you disembark at your destination station. Sounds complicated, but it seems to work even though local staff may not be entirely familiar with the process.

A direct service operated by TransPennine Express runs from Manchester to Windermere stopping at Kendal and Staveley along the way. Most of their trains have a dedicated area for carrying two bicycles and space can be booked in advance by calling Tel 0345 600 1674. Otherwise space is allocated on a first come first serve basis. See www. tpexpress.co.uk. There is also a route operated by Northern Rail that follows the Cumbrian coastline around the south and west of the region. These trains also carry a maximum of two bikes per train at the discretion of the conductor if the train is busy. See www.northernrail.org.

WOODROW WILSON ON WHEELS

There are a few connections between US presidents and Cumbria. The first, George Washington, was a direct descendant of the Strickland family that took its name from Great Strickland; the 12-year-old John Kennedy holidayed with his seven-year-old brother Robert at Killington in the late 1930s when their father was US ambassador to Great Britain; and Hillary Rodham rejected the first proposal of marriage from future husband Bill Clinton in Ennerdale in 1973.

US President Woodrow Wilson (1856–1924) who made five visits to the Lake District in the 'golden age' of cycling before World War I

But none was more enduring than that of keen cyclist Thomas Woodrow Wilson (1856-1924) who was the 28th President of the United States from 1913 to 1921. His mother, Janet, had been born in Carlisle, where her Scots born father, Dr Rev Thomas Woodrow, was a congregational minister from 1819 to 1835, when the family left for North America. Wilson is reputed to have been the first person to own and ride a bicycle in North Carolina.

He first visited Carlisle and the Lake District in 1896 but returned five times over the next 22 years. On his first trip, he disembarked at Glasgow and cycled to Carlisle, then took the train to Keswick and cycled to Grasmere. On his second tour in 1899, he cycled down from Glasgow to Dumfries, took the train to Penrith and then cycled down Ullswater, across to Keswick and on to Grasmere.

He visited the Lake District again in 1903 with his wife and again in 1906 with his daughters. Then in July 1909, he returned alone. After cycling from Lockerbie to Carlisle, he cycled through Penrith to Keswick and Grasmere, and then over to Coniston. He made his way by rail to Drigg, via Broughton in Furness, where he set off on a two-day ride around the Western Lakes, visiting Wasdale and Ennerdale. He stayed at Grasmere throughout the summer before going back to Glasgow on 2 September for the return journey.

By the time he made a last brief visit to Carlisle in 1918, he was the feted President of the United States and arrived on the royal train rather than a bicycle. The city celebrated its illustrious American cousin, but it is doubtful if Wilson enjoyed the experience. He made plans to return to the Lake District in 1921, travelling incognito with his second wife and her brother. However, his deteriorating health meant it never happened.

By bus

National Express, Britain's only scheduled coach network, say they may carry dismantled and folding bicycles if space is available provided they are suitably packed. They also state that carrying a bike on a service does not mean that they will carry it on any subsequent service. As this gives cyclists no reassurance that their bike will actually be carried yet alone any advice what to do with the transit box when they want to start cycling, they may as well say, 'No'.

Things do get better once you are in the Lake District. Stagecoach operates a number of summer services that are specifically equipped to carry bikes. The Lakeland Experience (Bowness–Ambleside–Grasmere) and

Cross Lakes Experience (Bowness–Hawkshead–Coniston–Grizedale) services in the central region can both carry two bikes, while the Bike Bus, which runs along the eastern shore of Windermere, can carry 12 bikes. See www.golakes.co.uk for details. Other bus services operated by Stagecoach only carry packed folding bicycles, but their long distance coaches carry non-folding bicycles in the luggage boot. See www.stagecoachbus.com for details.

WEATHER AND WHEN TO RIDE

The majority of tourists visiting the Lake District come by car so the roads can become very busy. Take the following into consideration to achieve

Heading off down Newlands Hause (Stage 3A)

an easier journey and a more enjoyable ride:

- Avoid national holidays and school holidays particularly those in July and August.
- Ride on weekdays rather than weekends when visitor numbers are swelled by day trippers.
- Ride early in the day before everyone else has risen or later when they are retiring indoors to eat.

Unless you have an entry to ride, you should also avoid the second Sunday in May when 2000 people test themselves riding 179km (112 miles) over the six big passes in the annual Fred Whitton Challenge.

The best time to go touring in the Lake District is between April and October, when the days are longer and the weather is at its best. But even then, you will undoubtedly get wet and experience blustery days. So be prepared for them. As a general rule always plan your route so that you are riding south to north with the prevailing south westerly winds. However, a circular tour or day ride will inevitably mean riding into the wind at some point and this is taken into account in this guide where the majority of the higher passes are ridden south to north and west to east wherever possible. However, check the weather forecast before you set out each day and be prepared to amend your plans to take account of the weather.

WHERE TO STAY

While many hardened cycle tourists prefer to camp, days of repeatedly ascending 1000m or more are unlikely to be pleasurable with a heavy load. This guide makes maximum use of the plethora of hostels and bunkhouses scattered across the region, but if you prefer additional comforts you will find a variety of accommodation to suit most pockets on www.GoLakes.co.uk, Visit England's official website for the Lake District.

You may not be able to get the type of accommodation you prefer close to the start or finish of each of the touring routes in this guidebook. Consequently, you may have to curtail your day before the end of a route, ride further into the next route or ride off the route and return the next day. For instance, the touring routes through the northeastern fells end at Troutbeck, where there are some B&Bs and a campsite. But if your preference is for hostels you would need to end your day earlier at Patterdale or Glenridding hostels, ride into the next stage and stay at the hostels at Scales, Keswick or Heskett Newmarket, or perhaps even make a detour to Penrith if everywhere else is full.

There may be lots of hostels, but there are also lots of hostellers, so it pays to book early. Hostels are always busy during the summer months and those in the more popular locations and along the route of the Coast to Coast (C2C) cycleway can be full at weekends, even in the depths of winter. The

Spiced apple pie with cream – and why not after all that effort?

Youth Hostel Association – www.yha. org.uk – has a number of hostels in the Lake District and there is an increasing number of independent hostels – see www.independenthostelguide.co.uk or similar for lists. There is also a growing number of camping barns, but you would need to carry a three-season sleeping bag as they typically only provide a mattress. Some barns lack cooking facilities and others have no electricity, so it is imperative to check the facilities of every barn before you book.

Many of Visit England's star-graded B&Bs, guest houses and hotels have enrolled with 'Cyclists Welcome' scheme and these are worth seeking out. Properties with the accreditation have drying facilities and bike storage and offer other services. Whatever you choose, if you want to arrive early to drop off your bike and go sightseeing or anticipate arriving later due to an unforeseen delay, it is only courteous to ring ahead and let them know. You should also remember that accommodation is in short supply and in the peak season even campsites can get full, so it is advisable to make a reservation as far ahead as possible. See Appendix B for a list of accommodation options.

WHAT TYPE OF BIKE?

Both touring routes and day rides can be ridden on any type of bicycle as there are no off-road sections that require a mountain bike. Routes follow quieter, secondary roads wherever possible. But as the region has a limited road network, main roads are used occasionally and you do need to be confident cycling alongside moving traffic.

Without wanting to offend the fans of tandems, tricycles, and folding and recumbent cycles, there are broadly three types of bike and all are suitable for the routes in this book. However, there are some things that you can do to make your rides more comfortable.

Road bikes

Touring bikes are usually made out of steel and have a longer frame than a normal road bike. This makes them springy and allows you to stretch out more. But there is nothing wrong with using a road bike for touring and all you really need to do is add a rack and fit the widest tyres that your wheel rims and frame clearance will allow. Most 'roadies' ride on 23mm tyres but moving up 25mm or 28mm tyres will give that extra bit of comfort and leave you less prone to punctures.

If your bike does not have threaded braze-ons, you will need to use a rack that clamps on to an alloy seat post. This is entirely adequate for lightweight 'credit card' touring. But if you are riding a bike with a carbon frame, you are probably best to try to go ultra-lightweight and limit yourself to frame bags or a single rack bag. And don't even think about clamping a rack to a carbon seat post. Buy a cheap alloy one instead.

Hybrid or city bikes

The only difference between road bikes and city bikes is normally the quality of the fittings and that most city bikes have flat handlebars. So in addition to fitting wider tyres, many people fit bar ends or even butterfly bars to give more choice in resting tired hands.

Mountain bikes

It is also worth considering fitting bar ends or butterfly bars to a mountain bike – and if your bike has full suspension you may need to fit the type of rack that clamps on to the seat tube. You might want to consider changing the knobbly tyres for lower profile urban tyres, which have less rolling resistance giving a far quieter ride. Locking off the suspension will also waste less energy when riding on good tarmac roads.

PREPARING YOUR BIKE

It is not a good idea to buy a new bike immediately before setting out on a touring holiday as new brake and gear cables will undoubtedly stretch and require fine tuning and you need time to become accustomed to the bike. You will be riding for extended periods of time, so it is very important that you adjust the bike to your size. The saddle is at the right height when there is still a slight bend in your knee when the pedal is at the bottom of the stroke. The way to check this is to place your heel flat on the pedal when it is at the bottom of the stroke and set the saddle height to this. Then when you put your foot on the pedal in a normal riding position with the ball of the foot centred on the pedal you should find your leg is still slightly bent. The handlebars should be level with, or just below, the height of your saddle but try a couple of positions until you feel comfortable. Riding for long periods can result in cramps in the hand, so consider adding bar-ends to flat handlebars and changing hand positions frequently. Having padded bars and cycling gloves with gel inserts in the palms all add to comfort, but remember to take each hand off the bars from time to time to flex and stretch the fingers too. One of the commonest aches suffered by riding for long periods of time is across the shoulders and occasionally in the lower back. The best way to prevent these is to pay attention to your posture, try to keep your upper body relaxed and to ride with your arms slightly flexed rather than locked on to the handlebars.

Unless the gears on your bike are suitable for the terrain you will be riding, you will find yourself struggling up any hills. It is always better to have a low gear in reserve than a high gear you never use and typically this means having a cassette with the largest sprocket having virtually the same number of teeth as the smallest chain ring – say a 28 or 30 tooth sprocket with a 34 or 36 tooth chain ring. However, if you explain where you are going to the folk at your local bike shop and tell them about the biggest climb you are likely to encounter, they will be able to fit the gears you need.

An obligatory cake stop in Great Langdale (Stage 5A and Route 2)

Laden for an autumn tour complete with a heavy DSLR, lenses and a tripod – since replaced by a light mirror-less camera

It is always advisable to have your bike serviced a couple of weeks before your trip, allowing sufficient time for any worn parts to be replaced and run-in before your departure. Some people will have the knowledge and tools to do this themselves; otherwise your local bike shop will be happy to do this for you.

- Wheels should run smoothly and show no signs of dishing or buckling. Check to see if there is any side-to-side play in the hubs or any missing or slack spokes.
- Tyres should be in good condition with plenty of tread left on them and no signs of weathering or weaknesses in the walls. They should also be inflated to the pressure recommended by the manufacturer as the less rubber there is in contact with the road, the easier

it will be to pedal. You should also remember that the Lake District is not just stone walls. Hawthorn is common in roadside hedges in the farmlands on the periphery of the national park and from midsummer onwards roads can be littered with thorny trimmings that easily cause punctures. For this reason tyres with a protective lining of Kevlar are essential – but, alas, still not infallible.

- Brakes should be effective with plenty of wear left on the brake blocks and room remaining for adjustment in the tension of the cables which should move smoothly and not show any signs of kinking or undue wear.
- Pedals and crankshaft should turn smoothly without any play in the axle.

- Gears should change smoothly and silently without the chain overriding the chain rings or sprockets when selecting high or low gears.
- All fixing nuts and bolts on mudguards and carriers should all be tight.

Even if there is nothing obviously wrong with your bike, apply oil to the chain and gears, check for loose spokes and excess play in brake and gear cables and have a short ride to make a final check that it's in tip-top condition before you leave home. If you do require the services of a bike shop on the road, see Appendix A for listings.

PREPARING YOURSELF

Unless you know how to use them, all the tools or spares you pack will be useless. So it pays to have at least one person in your party who can carry out the most common roadside repairs and do makeshift remedies for more major problems that will get you to the nearest cycle shop. Pack a small cycle maintenance manual as a backstop, but consider attending a cycle maintenance course as this will give you the hands-on skills you will be eternally grateful for when you find yourself fiddling with faulty gears in dwindling daylight.

To enjoy your tour and prevent each day from becoming a personal challenge, you should ensure that you attain a level of fitness that enables you to complete each day without becoming exhausted. As getting over the higher passes is physically demanding this may mean starting a personal fitness programme three or four months before your departure to give you sufficient time to build up stamina so you can complete the required distances and ascents comfortably. Start off with a ride that is just within your current fitness level and ride it a few times until you can ride it comfortably on two consecutive days. Then double the distance until you can ride the average daily distance needed for your planned tour without feeling unduly tired at the end of each day.

If you are going to encounter steep hills, practise 'feathering' the brakes – gently applying and releasing pressure on alternate levers – to control your speed on descents. It will prove invaluable when descending some of the steep Lakeland passes surrounded by moving traffic.

Carrying luggage, particularly a full set of panniers laden with camping gear, will slow you down dramatically. The accepted rule of thumb is that riding with a full load halves your average speed and comfortable daily range. So, regardless of what type of load you decide to carry, you should either do some laden training runs until you can achieve the distances needed for the tour or you should aim for training runs that are twice as long as you will cover on the tour. The first of these is perhaps the best choice as your bike will handle very differently when weighed down with a full set of luggage and it is better to get accustomed to this on quiet back roads before riding in traffic.

WHAT TO PACK

Climbing over the high passes is unlikely to be an enjoyable experience if you are weighed down by luggage. Fortunately the plethora of accommodation and high number of cycle shops for spares and repairs means you can keep the bike as light as possible. So here are some tips for lightweight touring in hilly terrain such as the Lake District:

- Think layers and add-ons rather than carrying a number of alternatives and only take one of each item of cycling clothing.
- Take two T-shirts and two sets of underwear and socks, but only one of each item of leisurewear.
- Consider cross-dressing. Meaning choose leisurewear, such as long-sleeved merino T- shirts, that can double as an extra layer for riding and a cycling waterproof that will suffice for chilly evenings.
- Make use of drying facilities to rinse through cycling gear and small items of leisurewear every evening – that's why you need two sets of some items of leisurewear; one on and one in the wash.
- Carry no more tools and accessories than you would on a day

ride and share them between the group.
- Buy travel-sized essentials such as shampoo and toothpaste and give shaving a miss for a week.
- Make do with a smartphone for all your communication and entertainment and leave all other electronics at home.
- Only carry one feed bottle – and replace the other with a storage bottle for tools and small accessories.
- A rear light is a year-round necessity as low cloud can result in poor visibility over the passes, but a front light is unnecessary during summer months.
- Virtually all hostels have secure bike storage so consider leaving heavy bike locks at home.
- Always wear a helmet. Riding without one alongside fast moving traffic on narrow roads bound by high stone walls that are just a few feet away is irresponsible.

Adopting such guidelines produces the kit list shown in Appendix C, which totals 5.4kg for short tours during the summer months and 6.8kg during winter when heavy leisurewear is needed for cooler evenings. Browsing through this list will also give some ideas for saving weight, such as leaving the Kindle at home and relying on the magazines and books typically found in hostels.

Investing in cycling shorts with a synthetic chamois insert will provide unparalleled comfort and prevent chaffing and sores. If you do not fancy shorts, you can buy full length cycling tights and if you don't fancy squeezing into body-hugging lycra, you can buy under-shorts that come with a chamois insert and simply wear comfortable clothing over the top. However, if you do start to get problems, apply talcum powder or an anti-fungal preparation at the first opportunity. Likewise, a good quality cycling jersey that wicks away perspiration and has a zipper at the neck to aid ventilation is another good investment.

HOW TO PACK

A large saddle pack is ideal for lightweight touring especially on a carbon frame (photo: Ian Gilbert)

Having reduced the kit list to 5.4kg or less, the next question is how to carry it. If you adopt the more traditional approach, you will be adding an additional 1600gm of weight for a pair of rear panniers and another 500gm for the rack meaning 28 per cent of the total weight carried is the luggage itself. Using a lightweight seat pack and a dry bag mounted between the handlebars using Velcro fastening systems such as those manufactured by Alpkit (see www.alpkit.com) and Apidura (see www.Apidura.com) reduces the weight of the carrying system to around 650gm – just 11 per cent of the total weight carried. While there are sacrifices in terms of volume and convenience, such systems are a realistic alternative for those preferring to travel light and those riding carbon-framed bikes. Others may prefer a more traditional saddlebag for lightweight touring.

If you are new to cycle touring one of the best ways to get to grips with packing is to pile everything you need to take in the middle of the floor and then try out a few different ways of packing. Remember to keep items you might need when you are riding easily accessible at the top of the kerb-side pannier and heavier items lower down wherever possible. Vulnerable items such as phones, cameras and maps need their own waterproof containers or bags and are best carried in a detachable handlebar bag where they are easily accessible. The same goes for money, credit cards and other valuables, which should never be left unattended on the bike.

Avoid having to ride with a rucksack or even a small water reservoir on your back as it will soon become uncomfortable and tiring. If you still need to carry a rucksack then it probably means that you have packed too much gear, so empty it all out and start again, looking to eliminate the non-essentials.

RIDING COMFORTABLY

If you do not currently hold a license for driving a vehicle of any kind, you should ensure that you are thoroughly familiar with the requirements of the Highway Code and consider attending one of the approved cycle training courses listed on the Cycle Touring Club website – www.ctc.org.uk. No matter where you go, you will find yourself having to ride along stretches of busy main roads and through town centres, where it is essential for both your own safety and that of others that you observe the Highway Code.

Riding in the wrong gear will soon start to cause aches and pains, particularly in the knees. The recommended cadence is in the range 70 to 90 revolutions per minute. You should try to maintain this rate all the time, constantly adjusting the gears to take account of the changing terrain. Pedalling in a gear that is too low is tiring and pushing against a gear that is too high is a primary cause of knee problems and one of the main reasons people abandon trips. If you start to feel any twinges in the joints, stop riding, check out your saddle height and riding position and pay

particular attention to your cadence when you resume. Similarly, try to avoid standing up on the pedals when you encounter hills and change down a gear or two until you are comfortable. If you have engaged your lowest gear and still find yourself needing to stand up to climb hills, it may be that your gearing range is too high for touring with a loaded bike, so call into the next cycle shop and hope they can fix it for you while you wait. Remember it is no disgrace to dismount and walk. Sometimes, such as when the weight of luggage causes the front wheel to lift on steep ascents, there is simply no other option.

Above all be flexible. Build some rest days and slack into your schedule so you can take a day off to do something else and perhaps sit out any bad weather. If the wind changes direction and you find yourself hopelessly battling against a headwind, either seek out an alternative route sheltered in the lea of higher ground, change plans and head off in another direction – or jump on a bus and start afresh tomorrow. It's not an endurance event; it's a holiday.

FUELLING YOUR RIDE

Cycling is strenuous and if you fail to keep your energy reserves topped up all the time by eating the right types of foods frequently, you will soon 'hit the wall' and feel very tired and demotivated. However, it is best to avoid starting the day with a

A fine display of bread at an artisan bakery in Grange-over-Sands (Route 15)

Autumn at the Kirkstile Inn at Loweswater, the brewery tap for Cumbrian Legendary Ales (Day ride 8)

food more frequently, so always have some favourite nibbles in your jersey pockets or handlebar bag. Likewise, carry water and drink frequently. It is also worth carrying sachets of isotonic powder to add to feed bottles in hot weather to replace vital salts and electrolytes.

Get into the routine of stopping frequently and taking a light snack rather than waiting until you feel hungry, as by then it is often too late. So, although there are plenty of places to stop and eat, always carry food with you. Many cyclists rely on things such as sandwiches, fruitcake, cereal bars and fruit. That is not to say, you should ignore the region's many inns and cafés, but err on the side of caution and stick to energy giving snacks and pastries rather than a full midday meal.

'full-English breakfast' as it will weigh heavy for most of the morning. It is far better to eat smaller amounts of

41

TEN FOODS TO TRY FROM THE LAKE DISTRICT

- Cumberland Rum Butter first appeared in the late 18th century using rum that was imported, or smuggled, through Whitehaven, Workington and Maryport by merchant ships trading with the West Indies. It became an established West Cumbrian treat and was adopted as an accompaniment to mince pies and Christmas pudding during the Victorian era.

- Cumberland Sauce is a fruit-based relish served with non-white meats, such as venison and lamb. It is not named after the county, having been created in Germany in honour of Queen Victoria's Hanoverian second cousin, the third Duke of Cumberland, sometime in the late 19th century. Since then it has been absorbed into Cumbrian cuisine as a local delicacy.

- Cumberland Sausage is a perennial favourite thought to have first been made in the 18th century when nutmeg, ginger and other spices were first shipped in to Whitehaven from the Americas.

- Damsons, grown in the Lyth and Winster valleys, are picked in September each year and used to make jams and puddings and to flavour gin.

- Grasmere gingerbread is made to a 'secret recipe' popularised by a domestic servant, Sarah Nelson (1815–1904), and is recorded as being a favourite of the poet William Wordsworth and his sister Dorothy.

- Herdwick Lamb mainly comes from the area around the Coniston and Duddon valleys where over 90 per cent of this hardy breed is reared. Look out for traditional Herdwick Lamb Cobbler on restaurant menus.

- Kendal Mint Cake was taken on the 1914–1917 Trans-Arctic Expedition under the command of Sir Edward Shackleton and on numerous expeditions to Everest, including the first ascent led by Sir Edmund Hillary in 1953, and rapidly gained a reputation as an energy provider.

- Morecambe Bay Shrimps have been caught by local fishermen along the coast for hundreds of years, first pushing nets by hand, then dragging nets with horses and finally tractors.

- Sticky toffee pudding was undoubtedly first created at a country hotel somewhere in the Lake District or Lancashire, but spread so quickly that no one is quite sure where. Today one of the largest and best-known manufacturers is located in Cartmel.

- Westmorland Pepper Cake is a distinctive fruitcake made with treacle and spiced with cloves, ginger and black pepper, which were all imported into Whitehaven in the 18th and early 19th centuries and bought in exchange for local wool.

RIDING AS A GROUP

If you are riding as part of a group, you should give special consideration to those around you, making them aware of obstacles such as pot-holes that they may not have seen and always alerting them to your intention to stop or turn by shouting out well before making the manoeuvre. It is only natural to ride two or three abreast on minor roads in order to chit chat, but the 'tail-end charlie' should remain alert to traffic coming up behind and instruct the group to revert to riding in single file or even pull over and stop until the vehicle has passed. This is particularly important when climbing over the high Lakeland passes where, unless you are super-human, you will be moving very slowly on narrow roads.

You should also look out for anyone who may be struggling and need a rest. If you get into the discipline of riding as a pack or peloton as professional racing cyclists do and take it in turns to go to the front for a few minutes at a time, it allows the others to take shelter in your slipstream. The benefits of doing this will vary with

Lambs on the road – another hazard to look out for in spring

conditions and the number of people in the group, but it is often said that cycling in a peloton increases the overall speed by 20 per cent to 30 per cent. It also gives respite to any member of the party who may be flagging, so it is well worth practicing.

CYCLE TOURING

Planning your trip
This guidebook describes a tour around the Lake District, with two alternative routes for each of the five stages described. The places that make up the start and finish points for each of these stages – Ambleside, Troutbeck, Keswick, Cockermouth and Eskdale Green – need not be where you decide to start or finish

your days riding, but they are places where decisions have to be made because the alternate routes diverge. Naturally you could decide to split the tour however you wish, as long as you can find somewhere to spend each night. Effectively, this gives a choice of thirty two variations of differing difficulty and length from 183km to 294km.

Choose your itinerary
This will depend on how many days you have available and how far you plan to ride each day. But you may have some other goals, such as climbing all the high passes or visiting each lake. Remember the Lake District is hilly and you need to be realistic about how far you will ride each day (see box).

Speeding past Fell Foot Farm after descending Wrynose Pass with the Langdale Pikes in the distance

ESTIMATING TIMES IN HILLY TERRAIN

Estimating how long a ride will take when it involves a significant amount of climbing is notoriously difficult. Hill walkers use 'Naismith's Rule' which allows one hour for every 3 miles (5km) covered in distance plus one hour for every 2000ft (600m) of ascent. Because there is considerable variation between the speed and climbing abilities of a committed club cyclist and a leisure cyclist, there is no comparable benchmark in cycling. However, the basic principle still applies: total time = time to cover the distance plus time spent ascending.

The Italian physician and cycling coach Michele Ferrari developed the term *velocità ascensionale media* (VAM) to refer to the average speed of ascent. VAM is usually expressed as metres per hour (m/h) and winners of mountain stages in grand tours typically climb at more than 1500m/h while most club cyclists are capable of climbing somewhere in the range 700–900m/h. In this book much more modest values have been used for VAM.

Estimated times for touring are based on 15kph plus 300m/h to account for the ascents. That means a ride of 60km with 900m of climbing would take seven hours.

Estimated times for day rides, where lighter bikes might be used and no luggage is carried, are based on 20kph plus 500m/h. So a day ride of 60km that involves 1000m of ascent is estimated to take roughly five hours.

To get an estimate of your own VAM, first assess your average speed on the flat and then record your times for a number of measured climbs and see what number best fits. But if all of this is too much for you, just use the rule of thumb, that 5 miles in the hills takes about as long as 8 miles on the flat.

Choose your start and finish points

Identify roughly where each day will begin and end and search for the most convenient accommodation that suits your budget. Inevitably this may mean amending your initial schedule giving some days when you ride less than you initially intended and others when you ride further, such as when you need to make a detour to your overnight accommodation. So be prepared to be flexible when it comes to accommodation; perhaps enjoying a night in a B&B if there are no hostels in the vicinity or vice versa.

Book your accommodation

Book your accommodation and finalise your schedule. You will have more choice about where to stay if you book your accommodation well in advance of your departure date – and that means months ahead if you are planning a tour during the busy summer months.

Touring the Lake District lakes

If your objective is to tackle all the high passes you can follow the route of the Fred Whitton Challenge (see below). Another option is to visit as many of the lakes as possible. The tour outlined below (in five-day and seven-day schedules) visits: Bassenthwaite, Buttermere, Coniston Water, Crummock Water, Derwentwater, Elterwater, Ennerdale Water, Esthwaite, Grasmere, Haweswater, Loweswater, Over Water, Rydal Water, Ullswater, Wastwater and Windermere. Thirlmere, which is technically a reservoir rather than a lake, is difficult to include in a circuit due to its central position. If you feel you must include it, an out-and-back diversion from Grasmere is recommended by back tracking part of Route 3. Visiting Haweswater also requires a 6km out-and-back diversion from Bampton.

TOURING THE LAKE DISTRICT LAKES

Five-day schedule

Day 1: Ambleside (Stage 1B) – Troutbeck (Stage 2A part) – Scales (86km)
Day 2: Scales (Stage 2A part reversed) – Troutbeck (Stage 2B) – Keswick (Stage 3B part) – Buttermere (75km)
Day 3: Buttermere (Stage 3B continued) – Cockermouth (Stage 4A) – Eskdale Green (YHA Hostel at Boot) (76km)
Day 4: Eskdale Green (Stage 5B) – Ambleside (57km)
Day 5: Ambleside (Route 2) – Ambleside (31km)

Seven-day schedule

Day 1: Ambleside (Stage 1B part) – Shap (42km)
Day 2: Shap (Stage 1B continued) – Troutbeck (Stage 2A part) – Scales (44km)
Day 3: Scales – (Stage 2A part reversed) – Troutbeck (Stage 2B) – Keswick (51km)
Day 4: Keswick (Stage 3B) – Cockermouth (44km)
Day 5: Cockermouth (Stage 4A) – Eskdale Green (YHA Hostel at Boot) (56km)
Day 6: Eskdale Green (Stage 5B) – Ambleside (57km)
Day 7: Ambleside (Route 2) – Ambleside (31km)

THE FRED WHITTON CHALLENGE

THE FRED WHITTON CHALLENGE

With the exception of 2001, when it was cancelled due to the foot-and-mouth epidemic, the Lakes Road Club has held the Fred Whitton Challenge every May since 1999 and it is now the 'must-do' sportive for every avid road cyclist. Seasoned riders view it as the ultimate day ride, while others will want to take it at a more leisurely pace; hence the reason for including it here sandwiched in between the touring routes and the day rides.

Named after Fred Whitton, a popular racing secretary of the Lakes Road Club, who died of cancer at the age of 50 in 1998, the primary purpose of the event is to raise funds for MacMillan nurses. The number of riders is limited, so priority is given to applicants who pledge to raise the most sponsorship. However, you can ride the Four Seasons Fred as a self-timed ride any time during the year, see www.fredwhittonchallenge.co.uk.

The official route is 179km (112 miles) and includes 3950m of ascent

THE FRED WHITTON CHALLENGE

Weekend schedule

Day 1: Ambleside (Stage 1A) – Troutbeck (Stage 2A) – Keswick (Stage 3A) – Cockermouth (99km)

Day 2: Cockermouth (Stage 4A) – Eskdale Green (Stage 5A) – Ambleside (91km)

Three-day schedule

Day 1: Ambleside (Stage 1A) – Troutbeck (Stage 2A) – Keswick (Stage 3A part) – Seatoller (61km)

Day 2: Seatoller (Stage 3A continued) – Cockermouth (Stage 4A part) – Nether Wasdale (85km)

Day 3: Nether Wasdale (Stage 4A continued) – Eskdale Green (Stage 5A) – Ambleside (44km)

Five-day schedule

Day 1: Ambleside (Stage 1A) – Troutbeck (Stage 2A part) – Scales (39km)

Day 2: Scales (Stage 2A continued) – Keswick (Stage 3A part) – Seatoller (22km)

Day 3: Seatoller (Stage 3A continued) – Cockermouth (38km)

Day 4: Cockermouth (Stage 4A part) – Nether Wasdale (47km)

Day 5: Nether Wasdale (Stage 4A continued) – Eskdale Green (Stage 5A) – Ambleside (44km)

Looking up to the Kirkstone Inn on the final section of The Struggle (Route 3)

and starts at the showfield in Grasmere (NY 342 076). Other than starting and finishing at Grasmere, following the C2C route through Loweswater rather than going into Cockermouth and skirting across the bottom of Wasdale, it is described in Stages 1A, 2A, 3A, 4A and 5A of the tour outlined in the first part of this guide. If it is ridden at the average touring speed used in this guidebook, it would take just over 24hrs and require overnight accommodation. If it is ridden at the average speed used for day rides in this guidebook (20kph and 500m/h), it would still be a long day of 16–17hrs.

Winners usually complete the course in less than six hours, which equates to riding at 50kph and climbing at 1600m/h, speeds that are up there with the professionals. And finishing as a tail-ender just within the cut-off times before the roads are reopened, means riding at 25kph and climbing at 800m/h. Others who prefer to ride at a more leisurely pace might want to try one of these schedules, which finish each day at a location where there is hostel accommodation.

DAY RIDES

If you simply want to do some cycling as part of a multi-activity holiday, then the day rides are for you. However, those touring should not ignore them as there is nothing better than taking a day out of an itinerary to enjoy some faster riding without the weight of panniers.

To keep the logistics easy for those with vehicles, all the day rides described in this guide are circular, beginning and finishing at the same place. To make access easier during busy weekends and holiday periods, many of these locations are on the periphery of the national park where parking is more easily available and cheaper. Being circular you can easily start and finish any of the day rides anywhere along the route. This could save you a few pounds in parking fees to say nothing of the hassle of tracking down an empty space.

Estimated times for day rides are based on 20kph plus 500m/h to account for the ascents. That means a ride of 60km with 1000m of climbing would take five hours. While you may feel you should be able to ride faster, do be conservative in estimating how long each ride may take, especially if family and friends are awaiting your return.

MAPS AND ITINERARIES

Although this book is designed for carrying on tour, it is still advisable to carry a separate map that covers your intended route. Many seasoned cycle tourists make do with a page from a road atlas or a printout from the internet while others carry Global Positioning System (GPS) with integrated mapping.

Unless you are planning to incorporate some walking, it is not necessary to take the Ordnance Survey

Approaching the summit of Corney Fell (Route 11)

1:50,000 Landranger Series; instead carry OS Travel Map 3, Lake District and Cumbria. This covers the entire district at a scale of 1:110,000, shows useful information such as hotels and public houses where there may be food and refreshments, and is more than adequate for making changes to your itinerary at short notice. If you have mapping software such as Memory-Map on your computer, or subscribe to a route plotting app, you can print out your intended route to any scale you wish and cut and paste a number of ribbon strips showing your route on a single side of A4 paper. If you laminate these back to back, you can often get your entire trip covering hundreds of miles on three or four totally weather-proofed sheets. You can even add text boxes containing the contact details of your accommodation. However these sheets do tend to catch the wind and it is advisable to punch a hole in the corners of each sheet and secure them to

the top of your bar bag. Alternatively, you can download everything to your smartphone.

The same goes for your itinerary. Download any travel timetables, accommodation details and contact numbers you need during your trip and cut and paste them on to an A4 sheet so they are legible but not over-large; you can get all the information you may have to refer to on a couple of sides. It saves having endless pieces of paper that blow away or get wet at the bottom of a pannier.

USING THIS GUIDE

The Lake District is a magnet for tourists with nearly 15 million visitors each year and in the summer the main roads are busy with a constant stream of traffic. Wherever possible the routes in this guide follow quieter country lanes and occasionally traffic-free trails. But inevitably there are some stretches where you will be cycling alongside faster moving vehicles. Coupled with the need to be descending steep inclines safely this means it is no place for novices and anyone lacking the skills or confidence to ride in traffic should look elsewhere.

Those provisos apart, riding in the Lake District is possibly the finest cycling that the UK can offer with challenging ascents amid wonderful scenery; it is undoubtedly why the Fred Whitton Challenge, is so massively popular. The rides that follow are divided into touring routes and day rides. Using the touring routes, you can plan your own itinerary with a couple of choices through or around each group of fells, while the day rides start and finish at the same location. Many will want to plan a holiday that combines both touring routes and day rides, staying in a location for an extra night so you can

enjoy a day of riding without being burdened by luggage.

Text and maps

There are 25 rides, each covered by separate maps drawn to a scale of 1:200,000 except maps in Stage 2A and Route 2 which are at a scale of 1:100,000. Place names on the maps that are significant for route navigation are shown in **bold** in the route descriptions. GPX files are freely available on the Cicerone website to anyone who has bought the book at www.cicerone.co.uk/778/gpx.

Each route description starts with an information box containing statistics to help choose which route or stage will best suit your level of fitness or cycling preferences: distance, climb, maximum gradient, approximation of time, grading (see below) and, where applicable, any major climbs. Some route descriptions offer alternative routes to avoid a busy

Near Sawrey, famous for its association with Beatrix Potter (Route 14)

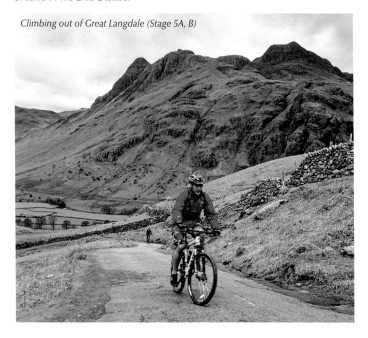

Climbing out of Great Langdale (Stage 5A, B)

stretch of road or a track unsuitable for skinny tryes, for example.

Grading

Each tour stage and day ride and is graded on two criteria: distance with rides categorised as short, medium or long, and total ascent with rides categorised as easy, moderate, hard or challenging.

- Easy – smooth pedalling with gentle inclines
- Moderate – undulating with an occasional steady climb, but nothing to get you out of the saddle

- Hard – involves some hard climbs with gradients up to 10 per cent
- Challenging – long steep ascents or multiple short sharp gradients that will most definitely hurt.

Inevitably, the majority of rides fall into the latter categories. You should note that climbs encountered on rides that use minor roads tend to have steeper gradients than those on major roads and consequently rides with a similar amount of climbing may have a different grading. Grades also become meaningless when riding into headwinds, when even the easiest ride will become much harder.

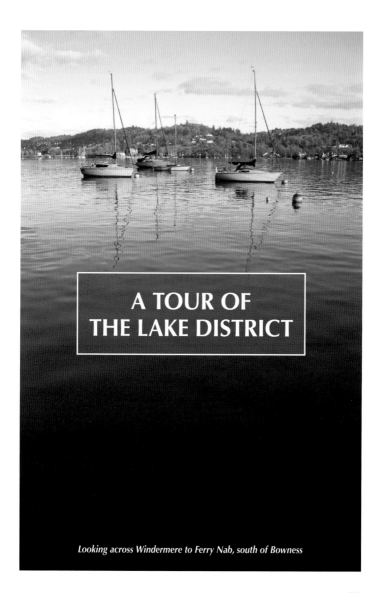

A TOUR OF
THE LAKE DISTRICT

Looking across Windermere to Ferry Nab, south of Bowness

THE EASTERN
AND FAR EASTERN FELLS

The Eastern Fells occupy the area between the A591 Keswick to Ambleside road and Ullswater to the east. The main spine of the group consists of Helvellyn and its neighbours in the north and the Fairfield group of fells in the south. There are also a number of outliers and subsidiary ridges, such as Striding Edge and Swirral Edge on the east of the main range making it a magnet for the more adventurous fell walkers. The Far Eastern Fells are to the east of Ullswater and Kirkstone Pass. Other than some dramatic, craggy fells surrounding the head of Haweswater, they are more rounded making for easier if less adventurous walking.

The road ends at the heads of the Kentmere and Longsleddale valleys that run deep into the Far Eastern Fells on their southern side and are just 6km away from the road end at the head of Haweswater. Linking these road ends by constructing a road over Gatesgarth Pass would require a considerable feat of civil engineering that would both open up these remote valleys and produce a climb of truly alpine proportions. Whether the conservation bodies would share the same enthusiasm for such a project is debatable.

So today the choice is between going over Kirkstone Pass between these two groups of fells or going right around the eastern border of the Far Eastern Fells, skirting along the boundary of the national park. Just like walking in these fells, the first is adventurous involving a hard climb followed by a helter-skelter descent, while the alternative is longer and through more remote countryside.

STAGE 1A

Ambleside to Troutbeck over Kirkstone Pass

Start	Ambleside (NY 377 044)
Finish	Troutbeck (NY 390 270)
Distance	35km (21 miles)
Climb	750m
Grade	Short/challenging
Time	4–5hrs
OS maps	90
Cafés/pubs	Ambleside, Troutbeck, Kirkstone Pass, Patterdale, Glenridding, Dockray, Troutbeck
Maximum gradient	12%
Major climbs	Kirkstone Pass: 9.6km, 388m, 12%

There are two villages called Troutbeck on this route, one near the beginning and one at the end, separated by Kirkstone Pass, which with an altitude of 454m is the highest of the Lakeland passes that is open to traffic. However, compared with the other Lakeland passes, the ascent from the south followed by this route is relatively gentle with a maximum gradient of 12 per cent.

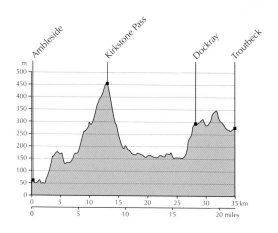

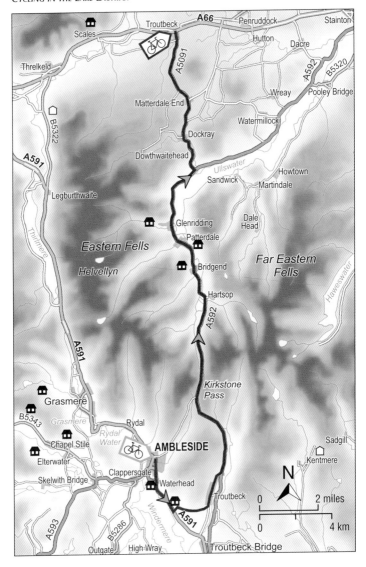

Ambleside has Norse origins meaning 'the sandy pasture by the river', but Ambleside did not stay pastoral for long. Its position at the hub of the Lake District on the packhorse route between Kendal and Keswick meant it became an important place for trading and in 1650 it was granted a charter to hold a weekly market. Besides wool and quarrying, the town was a centre for the production of charcoal, which was used in the iron industry during the 18th and 19th centuries. For the last 150 years, tourism has been the economic mainstay of the town.

Leave Ambleside on the **A591**, heading south towards Windermere. This road can be busy, but the route only follows it for a couple of kilometres before turning left towards Troutbeck up Holbeck Lane. There is no need to be disheartened at the sudden steepness of this lane, because it soon eases off and there is certainly nothing harder encountered on this route. Once around the corner, the view down the length of Windermere will soon lift flagging spirits.

TROUTBECK

Troutbeck was once on the stagecoach route between Windermere and Penrith and there are a number of drinking troughs bearing saints' names along the village street, which were for watering horses before they set out up Kirkstone Pass. These troughs are fed by wells and the presence of water is why the three hillside hamlets of Townhead, High Green and Townend, which make up the modern village, sprang up in the valley.

St James Well, one of a number of water troughs provided for thirsty horses passing through Troutbeck

Since the Middle Ages, the valley was a centre of the cloth industry with home workers turning fleeces into woven cloth. Evidence of this activity can still be seen in the spinning galleries on some of the older houses and in the remains of potash kilns on the Kirkstone Road, which produced soap for washing the cloth. This industry brought prosperity and the village has some fine examples of vernacular Lakeland architecture, particularly the statesmen's houses such as Townend House.

Beatrix Potter loved the village and in 1923 bought the 1900-acre Troutbeck Park Farm, which is down in the valley at the foot of Kirkstone Pass. Although it was never her main home, she oversaw the running of the farm and successfully bred a large flock of Herdwick sheep. When she died at the age of 77 in 1943, she left her property at Troutbeck (along with another 13 farms and her sheep) to the National Trust.

Being designated a conservation area in the 1960s also helps to protect this special village, which today has 26 listed buildings dating from the 17th, 18th and 19th centuries with the rest considered to be 'significant unlisted buildings'. Look out for the different types of 'bank barns', two-storey buildings sited on sloping ground with direct access from the ground to both levels.

The Kirkstone Inn, which was once an important coaching inn, claims to be the third highest public house in England.

Ride through **Troutbeck** to meet the A592 and turn left towards Kirkstone. It is a long unremitting climb, punctuated by a couple of false flats before a kilometre with an average gradient of 12–13 per cent up to the summit. ◄

If the climb had you shedding layers of clothing, it's time to zip up again for a fast, snaking descent to Brothers Water with lofty peaks on either side, including the eponymous Kirk Stone itself, high on the left just as descent begins. The surface is smooth and fast and you will revel at the opportunity to cash in some of the credits accumulated in the gravity bank on the ascent. Despite being back on the flat, the road alongside **Ullswater** is still fast but it pays to take a break at one of the many eating places in Patterdale and Glenridding as things are about to change.

It is just a short walk to either of the viewing points and you will be following in the footsteps of the poet William Wordsworth: he was a frequent visitor to the waterfall and mentions it in three of his poems.

After a few kilometres of undulating riding along the northern shore of Ullswater, turn left on to the A5091 towards Dockray. The road climbs gently with Glencoyne Park on the left and the ravine of Aira Beck with the 20m Aira Force waterfall below you on the right. ◄

The hotel at **Dockray** is the final opportunity for refreshments before the road climbs steadily up through the tiny hamlet of **Matterdale End** and across the open hillside around the squat cone of Great Mell Fell. Then, once clear of the conifer plantation, it is easy riding all the way to **Troutbeck**.

MV The Lady of the Lake berthed at Glenridding

STAGE 1B

Ambleside to Troutbeck via Shap

Start	Ambleside (NY 377 044)
Finish	Troutbeck (NY 390 270)
Distance	75km (46 miles)
Climb	1111m
Grade	Long/moderate
Time	8–9hrs
OS maps	90, 97
Cafés/pubs	Ambleside, Windermere, Staveley, Shap, Bampton, Askham, Pooley Bridge, Dacre, Whitbarrow, Troutbeck
Maximum gradient	8%

This stage goes around the Eastern Fells and the Far Eastern Fells, avoiding the steeper gradients. In the absence of suitable minor roads, the route uses some A roads. However, the A591 from Ambleside to Staveley has long stretches of traffic-free cycle path alongside the main carriageway and there are fewer vehicles on the A6 between Watchgate and Shap than on other main roads in the region.

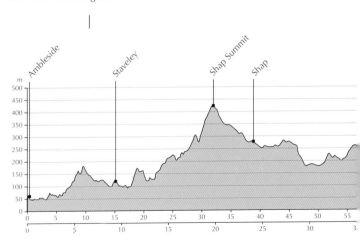

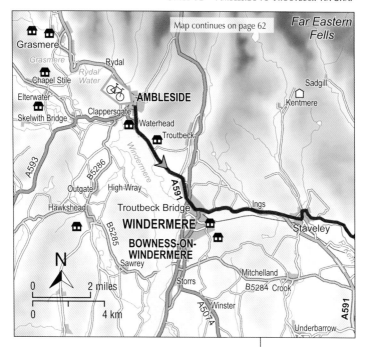

Map continues on page 62

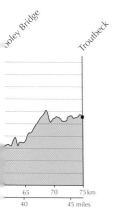

Leave Ambleside on the **A591**, heading south towards Windermere. This road is a main artery into the heart of the Lake District, but thanks to being adopted as part of the National Cycle Network, as NCN Route 6, there is a traffic-free path shared by cyclists and pedestrians once past Windermere. Turn off into **Staveley** and go through the village following the road towards Kentmere. ▶

Staveley Mill Yard, which once produced bobbins, is an interesting diversion housing galleries, workshops, creative studios, a micro-brewery and retail outlets including the UK's largest bike shop.

61

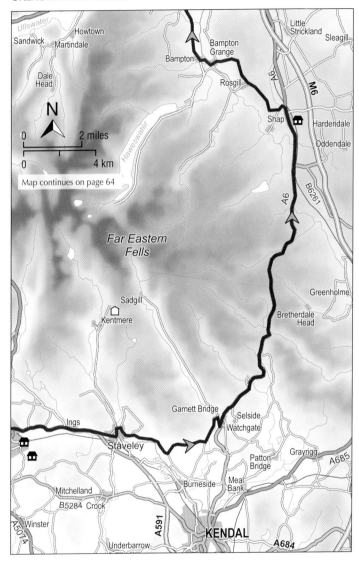

Map continues on page 64

Cross the **River Kent** towards Burneside and follow this road down the opposite bank. After 3km, turn left into a small lane at a junction in a copse of trees. The only sign here points back towards Staveley, but look for a white house beyond the wood. This road contours around Potter Fell and ends at a T junction with a metal gate in a stone wall. Turn left and ride to **Garnett Bridge**, a pretty village at the southern end of Long Sleddale. ▶

But stop singing and turn right towards Shap. The River Sprint drops sharply downhill to join the River Kent but the road goes uphill to meet the main A6. Turn left towards Penrith and ride for 19km with only the rolling countryside for enjoyment.

This stretch of empty road was the **main west coast route** between England and Scotland until the nearby stretch of the M6 motorway was opened in the 1970s. Truck drivers and others were frequently stranded in bad winter conditions and a slate memorial in a lay-by, 2km after Borrowdale Bridge, commemorates the local people who provided them with food and shelter. Another more

Garnett Bridge, the village that inspired Greendale where Postman Pat lives

Children's author John Cunliffe transformed it into Greendale, the home of Postman Pat and his black and white cat.

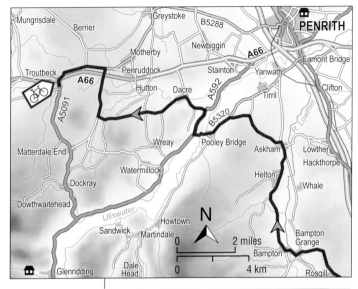

SHAP

After 350 years of domination by the Premonstratensian order of monks at the nearby abbey, which was founded around 1200 and fell into disuse after dissolution of the monasteries by Henry VIII in 1540, Shap had a renaissance as a staging post for those travelling between Scotland and England. This endured through the era of stage coaches and motor vehicles, bringing significant prosperity to

The impressive remains of the 15th-century tower at Shap Abbey

the village, right up until the 1970s when the opening of the M6 motorway left the village somewhat isolated. Free of the conservation constraints of the national parks either side of it, today quarrying for limestone and Shap blue and pink granites is the mainstay of the local economy.

notorious traveller in need of shelter was Bonnie Prince Charlie, who fought through snow, ice and mud over Shap Fell in the middle of December 1745 while retreating northwards to be finally routed at Culloden the following year. He will have followed the old road, which lies below the pylons in the plantation opposite Shap Pink Quarry, crossing Wasdale Beck by an old packhorse bridge which still stands.

At the top of **Shap** village, turn left towards Haweswater and ride through **Bampton Grange**, **Bampton** and **Helton** to **Askham**, which is a particularly attractive village that was once part of the Lowther estate. After the A6, this road is positively pastoral, with the River Lowther gently flowing through a flat valley surrounded by low rolling fells.

Just beyond Askham, turn left into a narrow road and ride through Celleron to the junction with the **B5230**. Turn left and ride through **Pooley Bridge**, turning right towards Penrith at the junction with the **A592**. Turn left at a sharp bend in the road and ride towards **Dacre**, turning left just before the village towards Sparket. Keep straight ahead at the crossroads heading towards the inverted pudding basin of Little Mell Fell. At the T junction at the end, turn right towards Dockray, and right again at the next T junction to meet the **A66**. Take the road opposite towards Greystoke, and then turn left at the T junction, eventually picking up the C2C cycle route that runs parallel to the A66 all the way to **Troutbeck**. ▸

The 14th-century Dacre Castle was built for protection against marauding Scots, but it is now a private residence and easily viewed from a nearby public footpath.

THE NORTHERN FELLS

Bound by the River Derwent on the west, the River Greta to the south and the River Caldew to the east, the Northern Fells are a self-contained group characterised by the absence of lakes. The area commonly known as 'Back o' Skiddaw' along their northern boundary gently declines to the Solway Firth with low hills and open moorland. But viewed from the south, the range from Skiddaw above Keswick along to Blencathra or Saddleback in the east forms an impressive vista.

Being entirely surrounded by roads, yet traversed by none, your only option as a cyclist is whether to go directly down into Keswick making use of quiet back roads and stretches of the Coast to Coast cycleway or go around the 'Back o' Skiddaw' on minor roads that skirt along the fells to give views across the Solway and into Southern Scotland. Unless you chose to overnight at the hostel at Scales or elsewhere along route, the former will take very little time at all being gently downhill for most of the way. Going around the 'Back o' Skiddaw' will take longer with the possibility of basic hostelling at Hesket Newmarket or staying in other accommodation along the way.

Many people will combine Stage 1A with Stage 2A or 2B and ride through the Eastern Fells and the Northern Fells in a single day. Others will want to allow more time to explore. Whichever is your preference, the Back o' Skiddaw comes highly recommended. It's a quiet part of the Lake District where you can lose yourself for a while.

STAGE 2A
Troutbeck to Keswick via Threlkeld

Start	Troutbeck (NY 390 270)
Finish	Keswick YHA (NY 267 235)
Distance	14km (9 miles)
Climb	76m
Grade	Short/easy
Time	1hr
OS maps	90
Cafés/pubs	Troutbeck, Scales, Threlkeld, Keswick
Maximum gradient	6%

Those on a tight schedule could easily combine this section with Stage 1A and ride from Ambleside to Keswick in a day. Those travelling at a more leisurely pace will find plenty of interest at Threlkeld Quarry and Mining Museum and Castlerigg stone circle. The latter involves a small diversion but the routes are virtually the same length.

On the quiet back road west of Troutbeck with Blencathra still topped with snow

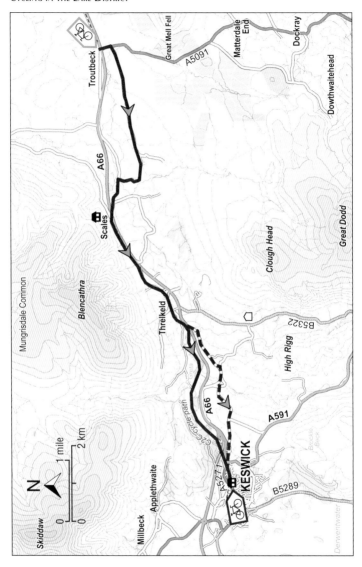

Leave Troutbeck on the small road signposted for Gill Head Campsite, just to the south of the village, and follow it all the way to Wallthwaite where it turns north between two farms to join another stretch of road that runs parallel to the main A66. ▶

On a clear day, there is a fine panorama of Blencathra with the serrated ridge of Sharp Edge clearly visible on its eastern flank.

Turn left and ride westwards to meet the A66. Cross the main road and follow the cycle path westwards towards Keswick. For a brief while this C2C path follows a loop of the old road in front of the White Horse Inn and Bunkhouse only to return to run alongside the road for another 2km before branching off between the trees and out on to a gated road to **Threlkeld**, where there is an excellent café behind the village hall.

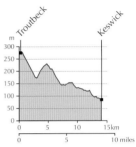

The area around **Threlkeld** was once an important centre for the mining of copper, lead, zinc and other mineral ores and for the quarrying of limestone, sandstone, granite and slate, which was all transported away on the Cockermouth, Keswick and Penrith Railway. The line closed in 1972 and stretches of the track have since been incorporated into the C2C cycle trail. However, you can still enjoy a short train journey on the 2ft (610cm) narrow gauge Threlkeld Quarry Railway, which is operated by the Threlkeld Quarry & Mining Museum.

Ride through the village and out the other side where the cycle path once again joins the A66. Continuing on the north side of the road, follow the cycle path along the old railway track alongside the **River Greta** soon arriving in **Keswick**. ▶

Those riding on skinny tyres are advised to take the alternative route past Castlerigg stone circle as there is less chance of a puncture on the coarse gravel railway track.

Alternative route via Castlerigg stone circle

Where the cycle path joins the A66 cross the carriageway and follow the quiet lanes that run past the site. The stone circle at Castlerigg was constructed in about 3000BC during the Neolithic period and is considered to be one of the most visually impressive prehistoric monuments in

Winter rainbow over Castlerigg stone circle | Britain with a backdrop of the dramatic Northern Fells. **Keswick** is reached shortly afterwards.

KESWICK

Meaning 'the place where cheese is made', Keswick shares its name with the West London borough of Chiswick, although with a trace of Scandinavian influence in the opening letter. Edward I granted the town a charter for a market in 1276 that continues today on Thursdays and Saturdays in the pedestrianised main street in front of the old Moot Hall, which was once the town hall but is now a tourist informa-

Street performers in Keswick town centre

tion office. Small-scale mining for graphite at Grey Knotts in the Honister Valley and a ready supply of timber provided the raw materials for the Derwent Cumberland Pencil Company to start producing the world's first pencils in 1832. Other manufacturers followed, but today all that remains is the Cumberland Pencil Museum, production having been moved out to Workington in 2008. Today the town thrives as the tourist centre of the North Lakes with a busy schedule of book and beer festivals throughout the year.

STAGE 2B

Troutbeck to Keswick via Hesket Newmarket

Start	Troutbeck (NY 390 270)
Finish	Keswick YHA (NY 267 235)
Distance	46km (29 miles)
Climb	620m
Grade	Medium/hard
Time	4–5hrs
OS maps	90
Cafés/pubs	Troutbeck, Mungrisdale, Hesket Newmarket, Bassenthwaite, Keswick
Maximum gradient	9%

There are some magical places around the perimeter of the national park and the Back o' Skiddaw is certainly one of them. This area of gently rolling hills and wild moorland to the north of Skiddaw and Blencathra is far less visited than the thronged towns and villages of the central Lakes with a quiet charm all of its own. Prepare to be captivated.

At the T junction at the northern end of Troutbeck, dismount and cross the main **A66**, then turn westwards along the unsigned quiet lane following the blue way-markers for the C2C cycle route. After 1.5km, where the lane joins the A66, continue following the C2C signs along the cycle path adjacent to the main road. ▶ Still following the C2C signs, turn northwards along a minor road towards Mungrisdale and Caldbeck.

In front of you is the distinct saddle-shaped ridge of Blencathra or Saddleback, the most easterly summit of the Northern Fells.

Continue all the way into **Mungrisdale**, leaving the C2C route at Beckside, where it crosses the strangely Scottish sounding River Glenderamackin. Keeping the fellside on your left and the flatter fields to your right, ride on through Bowscale and **Mosedale**. In the middle of Caldbeck Common, turn left, cross Carrock Beck and climb around the eastern flank of Carrock Fell to Calebreck before a pleasant descent into **Hesket Newmarket**. Turn

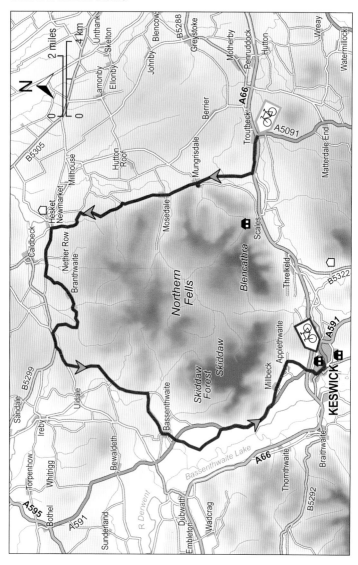

left into the village, up the broad main street, and out the other side following a narrow lane immediately to the left of Berkeley House towards Fellside and Branthwaite. After a short climb, turn left on to a smaller lane, still following signs for Fellside and Branthwaite.

Just after **Branthwaite** this road eventually turns into a track. Avoid that by turning right at a large agricultural shed and heading northwards to a T junction on the B5299. Turn left following directions for Keswick, which has clearly been added to this signpost as an afterthought. Near the summit of Aughertree Fell, turn left following signs for Orthwaite and Mirkholme, dropping down to Longlands before skirting around the western slopes of the Uldale Fells with first Chapelhouse Reservoir and then Over Water below on your right. You are now on Regional Cycle Route 38, which you follow all the way to Keswick.

The African explorer, **William George Brown** (1768–1813), who was murdered while travelling in Persia, is said to have owned, but never visited, the shocking pink hall at Orthwaite, which he inherited from a wealthy relative. And why is this adventurous traveller so unknown? Apparently even his contemporaries considered his writing to be deathly dull.

Orthwaite Hall, parts of which date from the 17th century

A kilometre south of the village, turn sharply right towards **Bassenthwaite**, dropping gently down through Park Wood. Turn left across the bridge and ride through the village, crossing the green beneath an avenue of trees. Turn left and then right, heading south towards the A591. Cross the main road taking an unsigned lane to the right of Chapel Farm that leads towards Scarness. At the end of this lane, turn left along the northern shore of **Bassenthwaite Lake**, then turn right at the T junction and follow the A591 towards Keswick.

After an absence of 150 years, **fish-eating ospreys** breed again at sites around Bassenthwaite Lake. They can been seen from viewpoints high up in Dodds Wood with wardens for the Royal Society for the Protection of Birds on hand during the breeding season from 1 April until 31 August each year.

Across the road is **Mirehouse**, a 17th-century house, built by the eighth Earl of Derby and owned by the Spedding family since 1802. During the 19th century, the family had strong connections

Spring at a hillside farm around the Back o' Skiddaw

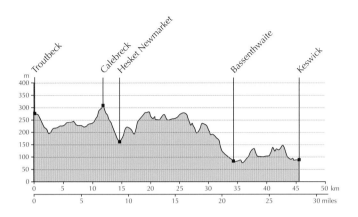

with poets, writers and painters, including William Wordsworth, Lord Alfred Tennyson, Robert Southey and John Constable, some of whom stayed at Mirehouse. Although still a family residence, parts of the house and its grounds are open to the public.

After 3km, turn left on to a minor road that runs along the foot of the fells passing through **Millbeck** and **Applethwaite**.

If you stop and look back across the lake to the ridge of the un-wooded **Barf Fell** you might catch a glimpse of a pillar of rock whitewashed to commemorate the drunken Bishop of Derry who died after falling from his horse following a wager that he could ride to the summit in 1789. It is said that the unfortunate horse is buried lower down the hillside.

When this road joins the A591 again, turn left, then cross the A66 at the roundabout and ride into **Keswick**.

THE NORTH WESTERN FELLS

Bounded by Bassenthwaite Lake and Derwentwater to the east and Crummock Water and Buttermere to the south and west, the North Western Fells form a tightly defined group including many, such as Cat Bells, Robinson and Grisedale Pike, that are perennial favourites of walkers. Roads run right around this group and bisect it twice climbing up through the valleys between the main ridges that predominantly run west to east. This terrain means it is the area of the Lake District that contains the greatest number of high passes: Honister Pass on the southern perimeter, Newlands Hause which cuts through the southern end of the group and Whinlatter Pass which cuts through the northern end of the group.

The shortest alternative here simply tracks around the eastern and southern border of this group climbing Honister Pass before continuing through the gentler Lorton Vale to reach Cockermouth. But the alternative, which loops back to take in Newlands Hause and then Whinlatter Pass, only adds another 7km and an extra 300m of ascending. So given the small amount of extra effort involved for two additional glorious descents, it's the longer route every time for me. If both of these stages seem like too much hard work, then follow National Cycle Route 71, which runs alongside the main A66 all the way from Keswick to Cockermouth.

If you are following the flow of this guidebook and planning an anti-clockwise tour around the Lake District using hostels for accommodation, be aware that there are few that are convenient for cyclists until towards the ends of Stages 4A and 4B. Therefore, unless you are untroubled by a long day in the saddle, you should stay at the YHA Hostel in Cockermouth or other accommodation in or near the town.

STAGE 3A

Keswick to Cockermouth over the passes

Start	Keswick YHA (NY 267 235)
Finish	Cockermouth YHA (NY 118 298)
Distance	51km (32 miles)
Climb	1085m
Grade	Medium/challenging
Time	6–7hrs
OS maps	89
Cafés/pubs	Keswick, Rosthwaite, Seatoller, Honister, Buttermere, Braithwaite Cockermouth
Maximum gradient	25%
Major climbs	Honister Pass: 2.3km, 253m, 25%; Newlands Hause: 1.9km, 205m, 25%; Whinlatter Pass: 3.3km, 231m, 15%

If you are intent on bagging all the high passes then this route, through the North Western Fells, is essential as it includes Honister Pass, Newlands Hause and Whinlatter Pass, all of them classic Lakeland climbs.

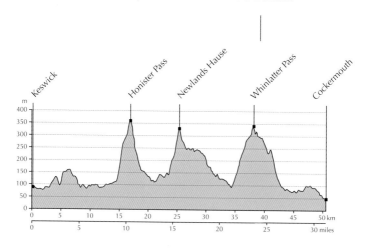

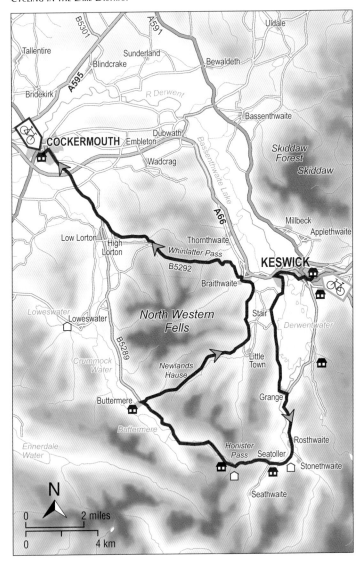

From the centre of Keswick, head up Main Street over the River Greta and follow road signs for North Cumbria West A66. Once on the outskirts of the town, turn left, following way-marker signs for the C2C cycle path and cross the bridge over the River Derwent. After a kilometre, we leave the C2C path as it drops down into the woods on the north side of Swinside and continue straight on following signs for Grange.

> Tucked away in the woods on the shore of **Derwentwater** are two mansions, Lingholm and Fawe Park, where the young Beatrix Potter spent nine family holidays sketching and painting scenes that would later appear in her stories, such as a vegetable garden that inspired Mr McGregor's Garden in *The Tale of Peter Rabbit*.
>
> Derwentwater is also the last known home to Britain's rarest fish, a small white deepwater fish called the vendace, which is more widespread in North Europe.

Caught in a shower on the south side of Derwentwater

Ignore signs for Buttermere for the moment and take the turnings for Grange at each of the next few junctions to end up on a narrow road with woodlands on your left and the slopes of Cat Bells on your right. It is glorious cycling with an almost imperceptible gain in height that allows fine views out over Derwentwater. After a slight downhill, it's out into the open pasture at **Grange**. ◄ A fine double-arched stone bridge spans the River Derwent and leads to the B5289, which is the main road through Borrowdale.

In medieval times, the monks of Furness Abbey farmed here, giving this pretty village its name.

Turn right at the junction heading towards Seatoller. The road writhes beside the river through the narrow 'Jaws of Borrowdale' with Castle Crag to the right and Grange Fell on the left before opening out on to fields at **Rosthwaite**. Following the path of the valley, the road swings around to the west to **Seatoller** and its satellite **Seathwaite**, which is reputed to be the wettest place in England with an annual rainfall of 3.15m (125in).

MANHUNTS IN BORROWDALE

While staying at Seatoller in Borrowdale in June 1898 when they were Cambridge undergraduates, the historian Geoffrey M Trevelyan, pioneering rock-climber Geoffrey Winthrop Young and Sidney McDougall organised 'The Lake Hunt'. This was a masochistic version of hide and seek specially adapted for the Lakeland Fells that was inspired by Robert Louis Stevenson's great manhunt in his novel *Kidnapped*. The objective of the game was for the two pairs of 'Hares', who had been deposited by a neutral umpire at widely separated locations unknown to each other to meet up before the 20 or so 'Hounds' caught sight of their red sashes and captured them. A single game lasted for three or four days and nights with the 'Hares' hiding in caves, disused mines and barns between hair-raising chases down rough fell sides and scrambles up rocky crags.

With breaks only during war years, the hunt has continued for over 100 years. Today the Trevelyan family and their friends hold an event in Borrowdale at Whitsun and the Trinity Hunt takes place every June organised by alumni who just cannot bear to give it up. Co-founder, Sidney McDougall, sadly had that choice made for him when he was killed fighting at Gallipoli in 1915.

After miles of easy rolling, it's time to build up some credits in the gravity bank by climbing Honister Pass. Ridden from the other side as Simon Warren did for his book *100 Great Cyclist Climbs*, the overall gradient is seven per cent with two stretches above 20 per cent. But from this side the overall gradient is 10 per cent, with only one short stretch above 20 per cent. The transition from the valley floor to the slope comes suddenly and the steepest section comes early just as the road clears the tree line. But after that the gradient eases off, the views open out and there is the prospect of a well-earned treat in the café at the summit to focus the mind.

Westmorland green slate has been quarried at outcrops around Honister since the 17th century. Demand increased in the 19th century when the boom in house building in the Lancashire mill towns led to an increase in demand and tunnels were dug under both Yew Crag and Honister Crag to access underground seams. In the early days teams of packhorses hauled sleds laden with the finished slate down narrow paths that traversed the crags, but over the years these were replaced with an aerial ropeway and eventually a narrow gauge, petrol driven locomotive. A succession of owners struggled to make production commercially viable throughout the 20th century. However, since the site was turned into a tourist attraction, small amounts of slate are still produced.

Once over the top, it's time to make a withdrawal from the gravity bank with a 3km descent. But take particular care to keep your speed under control as the gradient of the first kilometre is more than 20 per cent. Once on the valley floor, it is easy pedalling again alongside **Buttermere**. Just before the village, turn sharp right to climb **Newlands Hause**. Whoever built the road chose a good line as the steepest sections are broken by flatter stretches where lungs and legs can recover, before tackling the very steepest gradient where the road zigzags just before the summit.

Approaching the summit of Newlands Hause on a wet autumn day

Whinlatter is England's only true mountain forest and has stunning views, wildlife such as red squirrels, plenty of outdoor activities on offer and a visitor centre with café, cycle shop and gift shop.

Take a few minutes to give disparaging looks to any walkers who have used their vehicles to get them high into the fells with zero effort, then cash in the gravity credits and enjoy the descent, remembering there are some sharp corners ahead at Keskadale Farm. Follow the signs for Braithwaite, keeping high above the valley with the fells immediately to your left. Ride through **Braithwaite** and turn left at a crossroads alongside the Royal Oak Inn. This is the start of **Whinlatter Pass**, which starts as a gentle ascent up through mixed woodland, but gets progressively steeper as you approach the viewpoint that looks out over Bassenthwaite Lake. After that, the gradient eases with a long straight ramp up to the visitor centre at the summit. ◄

Ignore any signs for the C2C cycle trail on the descent and stick with the B5292 through **High Lorton**. Turn right following the B5289 all the way into **Cockermouth**. For directions to the Youth Hostel, see Stage 3B.

STAGE 3B

Keswick to Cockermouth via Lorton

Start	Keswick YHA (NY 267 235)
Finish	Cockermouth YHA (NY 118 298)
Distance	44km (28 miles)
Climb	794m
Grade	Short/hard
Time	5–6hrs
OS maps	89
Cafés/pubs	Keswick, Grange, Rosthwaite, Seatoller, Honister, Buttermere, Low Lorton, Cockermouth
Maximum gradient	25%
Major climbs	Honister Pass: 2.3km, 253m, 25%

Riding through the unmissable Borrowdale and Buttermere valleys involves climbing over Honister Pass, so pace yourself and be ready to get off and push. Flatter alternatives between Keswick and Cockermouth would be to follow the low-level option of the C2C cycle path – NCR 71 that runs parallel to the A66 or to reverse Stage 2B to Kilnhill and follow Route 9 into Cockermouth. However, the scenery along both of these alternatives is nothing compared with that of the route described here.

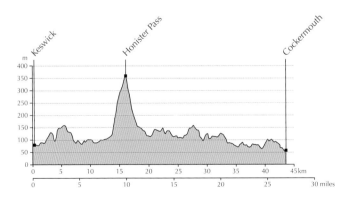

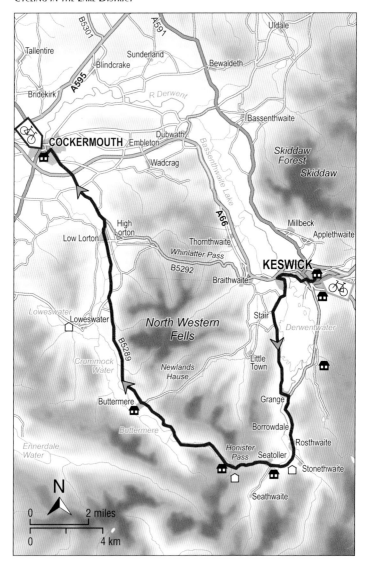

Starting the descent of Honister Pass

The route follows Stage 3A until **Buttermere**. ▶ Cycle through the village, then alongside **Crummock Water** all the way to Brackenthwaite. At the T junction turn right following signs for Lorton and Cockermouth. Ride through **Lorton** and keep following the B5289 all the way into **Cockermouth**. For the Youth Hostel, follow the A5086 southwards towards Egremont and then the signs for Youth Hostel from the end of Gallowbarrow.

A window in St James' Church, Buttermere, commemorates the guidebook writer Alfred Wainwright (1907–1991) whose ashes are scattered at his favourite spot on Haystacks across the lake.

COCKERMOUTH

Its position at the confluence of the River Cocker and River Derwent has left Cockermouth prone to dramatic flooding. The town was granted charters to hold markets by Henry III in 1221 and again in 1227, but its location meant it was an important centre for trading well before those dates. Before licensing laws were relaxed, holding markets on more than one day and on special holidays allowed the public houses to open and Cockermouth became an important destination for those in the vicinity who enjoyed their ale. It was perhaps this reputation for drink and revelry that influenced those planning the national park to map the boundary tightly around the east of the town, forever relegating the town to the second division when it comes to tourism. This is a pity because the town is a little gem with lots of history.

The birthplace of William Wordsworth in Cockermouth

The Normans built Cockermouth Castle close to the river crossing, but after being routed by Robert the Bruce in 1315 and dismantled by the Parliamentarians after the English Civil War in 1640 little remains of it today. It was its importance as a place of commerce and manufacturing during medieval times that shaped the town with its broad main street of merchants' houses, each with its own plot stretching to a 'back lane'. There were mills processing wool, linen and cotton, tanneries, chair makers and all sorts of workshops making everything from nails to hats.Parts of the town, such as the tree-lined Kirkgate, were rebuilt in the Georgian era with classical late 17th- and 18th-century terraced housing, but behind these facades, twisting cobbled lanes run steeply down to the river. Careful restoration and renovation of the Market Place and the surrounding central area has protected this rich architectural heritage making Cockermouth a wonderful place to visit.

Best known as the birthplace of the poet William Wordsworth (1770–1850) and his sister Dorothy (1771–1855), other famous residents of Cockermouth include John Dalton, (1766–1844), the father of atomic theory, Fletcher Christian (1764–1793), who led the mutiny on 'HMS Bounty', and the Irish nobleman Lord Mayo (1822–1872), who was the local MP from 1877–1868, before becoming Viceroy of India. He was assassinated by an aggrieved convict while inspecting a prison in the Andaman Islands in 1872 and is commemorated by an imposing statue at the bottom of the main street.

THE WESTERN FELLS

The Western Fells are bounded by Wastwater to the south and Buttermere, Crummock Water and Loweswater to the north forming a compact triangular group. The wild and rocky character of the eastern summits in the group diminishes to the west until the fells merge seamlessly into the coastal plain. Paths run along the valley bottoms and over the high passes but, unfortunately, there are no roads so the only option for cyclists is to ride around their western edge.

The shorter option here follows the boundary of the national park for much of the way taking in a climb up Burn Edge, which gives fine views over the towns and villages along the coast and out across the Irish Sea, before turning west to Wasdale and Eskdale Green. The longer option stays further out on the flatter coastal plain and follows the course of the River Ehen to Egremont then turns east and merges with the shorter option for the final stretch to Eskdale Green.

Heading through the Eskdale Valley below Harter Fell

STAGE 4A

*Cockermouth to Eskdale Green
via Ennerdale Green*

Start	Cockermouth YHA (NY 119 308)
Finish	Eskdale Green (SD 142 002)
Distance	56km (35 miles)
Climb	897m
Grade	Medium/hard
Time	6–7hrs
OS maps	89
Cafés/pubs	Cockermouth, Ennerdale Bridge, Calder Bridge, Gosforth, Nether Wasdale, Santon Bridge, Keyhow, Eskdale Green
Maximum gradient	10%
Major climbs	Burn Edge: 3.5km, 184m, 12%

Do not let the ascent up Burn Edge deter you from taking this option. It is a favourite climb of riders from clubs based in West Cumbria and is listed in Simon Warren's *Another 100 Climbs*. However, the gradient is fairly uniform throughout and only briefly gets into double figures.

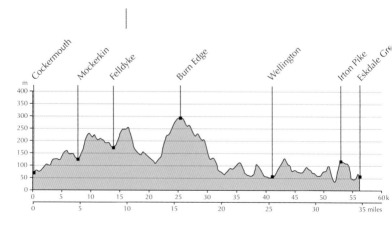

Follow the A5086 southwards along Lamplugh Road and across A66 at the roundabout following signs for Egremont. After 2 km turn left at Eaglesfield Primary School towards Lorton and Embleton, then right towards Brandlingill. At the T junction, turn south towards Mosser. Until now it is easy rolling, but there is a short little climb out of Mosser and the road continues to undulate through Sosgill all the way to **Mockerkin**. Turn left at the crossroad as you enter the village, following signs for Loweswater and Ennerdale and left again at the T junction following signs for Loweswater and Buttermere. The road climbs up over Mockerkin Howe gradually revealing views of Loweswater below. At the T junction at Fangs Brow, turn right towards Lamplugh.

Chances are you will meet other riders along this stretch of road crossing from the Irish Sea to the North Sea on the C2C cycleway and you can follow the C2C way-markers all the way through **Lamplugh**. Leave the C2C where it turns right towards Kirkland and go straight ahead towards Croasdale, with some good views towards Ennerdale Water and enjoyable downhill riding

Heading through the beech trees towards Mosser

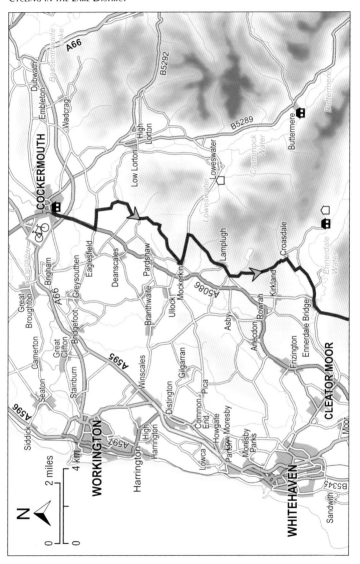

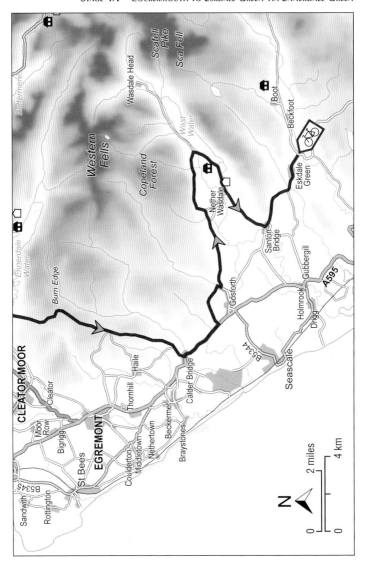

Riders from one of the many local cycling clubs putting in the miles on a winter afternoon

through the sweeping bends. Turn right at the T junction in **Croasdale** and follow the road as it weaves its way to **Ennerdale Bridge**, with the option of making a short diversion down to the shore of Ennerdale Water along the way.

ENNERDALE

Although a natural lake formed by glacial action, the addition of a small weir at its western end in 1902 to guarantee a constant supply of water for the then booming town of Whitehaven means Ennerdale Water is a hybrid between a lake and a reservoir. Due to the lack of vehicular access the valley remains relatively unspoilt by tourism and there is a program of 're-wilding' the area to correct some of the over-zealous conifer planting done in the middle of the last century. Its remoteness and the impressive cirque of rocky fells at the head of the valley make it a special place; former US president Bill Clinton certainly felt that way as he chose it as the spot to propose to Hillary in 1973.

There are two YHA hostels in the valley: Gillerthwaite, which is 4 km up a forest track beyond the road end at Bowness Knot car park, and Black Sail Hut, which is nearly 300m above sea level at the head of the valley. Neither is accessible on skinny road tyres, although you could easily ride to Gillerthwaite on a bike fitted with chunky tyres.

Turn left at the T junction towards Cleator Moor and then, just beyond the outskirts of the village, turn left up **Burn Edge** towards Calder Bridge and Gosforth. The open road climbs steadily upwards at a six per cent gradient, passing Blakeley Raise stone circle, to reach the highest point of the route at 280m above sea level.

> This is exactly the type of place you would expect to find a **stone circle**, in a glorious position with views in all directions. But as the stones are cemented into position, no one is quite sure whether it is a genuine antiquity that was badly restored back in the 1920s or a complete fake.

Now with the hard work done, there is 8km of descent to enjoy with views over the Irish Sea on a clear day.

Towards the bottom there is a steeper section with a 20 per cent gradient before a flat run in to reach **Calder Bridge**. Turn left on to the A595. ▶ After 3km, turn left at Boonwood Nursery into an unmarked road that leads uphill before turning right and dropping sharply down into Wellington. This village is a satellite of Gosforth Bridge but unless you need supplies, turn left at the T junction and climb steeply out of the valley towards Nether Wasdale and Wastwater Head.

This is a pleasant lane, but glimpses of the Wasdale Screes ahead promise much more dramatic scenery just around the corner. So ignore the signs for Nether Wasdale and continue all the way down to **Wast Water** for a closer view before turning south towards **Nether Wasdale** along the valley road.

> Retracting glaciers trapped in the steep sided valley of **Wasdale** 'over-deepened' Wast Water to create England's deepest lake with a depth of 79m; some of it well below sea level. Its depth makes it attractive to sub-aqua divers who are rumoured to maintain a gnome garden more than 50m below the surface.
>
> UK rock climbing has its origins as a sport on the crags that surround the head of the valley when

At peak times, it can be a busy road: you could ride the National Cycle Route 72 between Sellafield Station and Seascale but with heavy panniers or on skinny tyres it's tough riding.

Heading towards Wasdale Head with the summit of Kirk Fell standing out above the cloud

undergraduates holidaying at the Wasdale Head Hotel started exploring the fells in the 1880s. With only rough hawser-laid ropes and little in the way of protection, their notebooks show they frequently resorted to 'combined tactics' – standing on the another's shoulders – to overcome difficult pitches; something that would be deeply frowned upon by today's free-climbers.

Turn left at the T junction and up through the woodlands to **Santon Bridge**. Then turn left again at the junction in the village following signs for Eskdale. There is a final short climb around Irton Pike. It may not be that arduous but it claimed the life of William Malkinson, who according to *The Whitehaven News*, 'expired with terrible suddenness' on 21 February 1886 while on his way to preach at the Wesleyan chapel in Eskdale. Look out for the small memorial stone that marks the sad event.

THE JAPANESE GARDEN AT ESKDALE GREEN

The Japan-Britain Exhibition of 1910 sparked a huge interest in all things Japanese and triggered James Rea, who had built the nearby mansion of Gate House in 1896, to commission the local landscape architect Thomas Mawson to create a Japanese garden for him in a wood known as Giggle Alley. Rea, who ran the Liverpool branch of his family's hugely successful coal and shipping business, was an enthusiastic plant collector and Mawson owned Lakeland Nurseries near Windermere and had already created gardens for many local properties including Brockhole, Holehird, and Rydal and Holker Halls. It was a coming together of like minds with deep pockets.

At its height the garden was obviously magnificent but over the years the Outward Bound Trust acquired Gate House and the Forestry Commission purchased Giggle Alley, and the garden became neglected and overgrown. However, after being caringly restored by local volunteers and Forest Enterprises, the garden is once again a stunning place to visit with dense thickets of bamboo, a collection of mature Japanese maples and the heady aroma of azaleas in the spring.

STAGE 4B
Cockermouth to Eskdale Green via Egremont

Start	Cockermouth YHA (NY 119 308)
Finish	Eskdale Green (SD 142 002)
Distance	65km (41 miles)
Climb	792m
Grade	Medium/moderate
Time	6–7hrs
OS maps	89
Cafés/pubs	Cockermouth, Brigham, Rowrah, Calder Bridge, Gosforth, Nether Wasdale, Santon Bridge, Keyhow, Eskdale Green
Maximum gradient	8%

This flatter alternative around the Western Fells takes the quiet roads through the coastal plain to avoid the climb at Burn Edge before joining Stage 4A just before Calder Bridge for the final few miles.

Leave Cockermouth town centre following signs for Whitehaven and Workington. After crossing the A66 at the roundabout, take a tarmac path on the left. It soon turns into a road, which skirts around the north side of

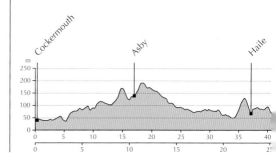

'When I was a lad' – a sculpture in Egremont commemorating the mining heritage of the area by local artist Colin Telfer

Brigham to Broughton Cross. Once through the village, turn left to Greysouthen, where a left turn at the top of a short hill in the centre of the village leads to **Dean**. Turn right at a T junction in the centre of the village and ride to Ullock, where the route turns right towards Branthwaite and then left to Dean Cross with the River Marron bubbling away below the road on the left. The low hills of the Western Fells lay a couple of miles away to the east.

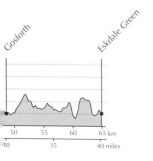

Turn left at the lonely crossroads towards Alecdon and follow this road through **Asby** to the old industrial village of **Rowrah**. Join the A5086 heading westwards towards Egremont but within 500 metres turn left towards Rowrah Hall to pick up the C2C

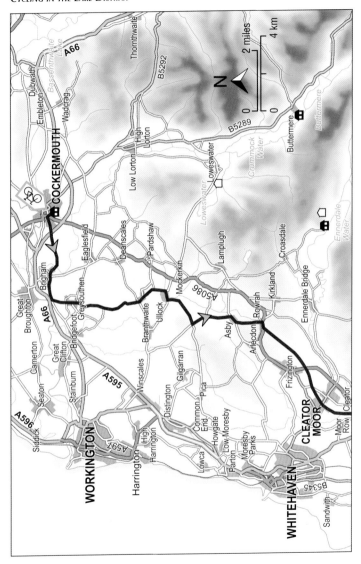

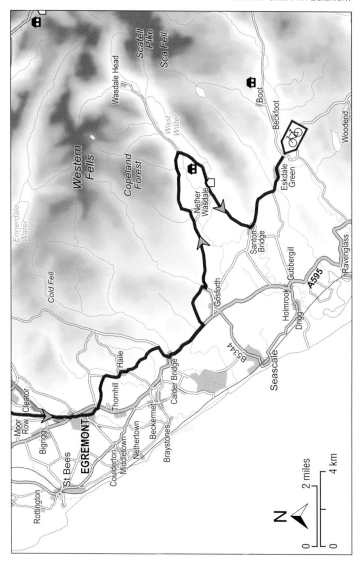

Before it closed in 2008, Egremont's Florence Mine was the last working deep iron ore mine in Europe, producing haematite for cosmetics and jewellery; today it's an arts centre.

cycleway, National Cycle Route 71. Follow this westward towards Whitehaven for 7km, taking care not to collide with any dogs or their owners along the way. Then just beyond **Cleator Moor**, turn left on to National Cycle Route 72 and follow it right through to **Egremont**. ◄

Abandon NCR72 at the southern tip of the town and cross the roundabout at the A595 following signs for Haile. Once in **Haile** turn right towards Beckermet, then left into an unmarked lane at the end of the village. After 2km this lane drops sharply to join Stage 4A. Follow the description for that route into Calder Bridge and all the way to Eskdale Green.

CLEATOR MOOR

The artist LS Lowry (1887–1976) visited Cleator Moor frequently during the 1950s and used the town as inspiration for his paintings of industrial life. There was simply nowhere better as Cleator Moor was built on heavy industry. The town sprang up in the 19th century on the back of several coal and iron ore mines with a huge influx of workers from all parts of the UK and so many from Ireland that the town gained the nickname 'Little Ireland'. The need for labour during World War I and World War II saw a fresh influx of immigrants from mainland Europe and today the area has a diverse cultural mix.

At its height, Cleator Moor was served by two railways which carried ore away to be processed elsewhere. But by the early 1900s much of the ore had been worked out and the coal was becoming too expensive to mine. During the 20th century, sections of the track were closed until, by the end of the 1990s, nothing was left. Thankfully the arrival of the Sellafield complex absorbed some of the unemployment that resulted from the decline of traditional industries, although creating employment has remained a struggle for decades. The old railways fared better, having been put to good use as National Cycle Routes providing gentle and traffic-free cycling. Sculptures along the way celebrate the industrial heritage of the area.

Approaching Cleator Moor on National Cycle Route 71

THE SOUTHERN
AND CENTRAL FELLS

The Southern Fells occupy an area bounded by Wastwater in the west, Borrowdale in the north and Great Langdale and Coniston Water to the east. Alfred Wainwright himself made an arbitrary judgement about the southern boundary and ignored the area south and west of Green Crag as he considered the scenery inferior. Then again he was no cyclist and could not be expected to be looking out for challenging climbs and exhilarating descents.

Scafell Pike, Scafell and Bowfell dominate the northern part of this group making it the highest terrain in England and there is not a road crossing until Hardknott Pass and Wrynose Pass link Eskdale with Langdale. To the south, the roads run predominantly north to south so that avoiding the harder passes means a longer ride southwards across Dunnerdale before returning northwards along Coniston Water.

The Central Fells, which are lower than the surrounding hills, occupy the area bounded by Derwentwater and Borrowdale to the west, Thirlmere to east and Great Langdale to the south. There are no roads through the group.

At Eskdale Green your choices are climbing over the Hardknott and Wrynose passes in quick succession before finishing with a pleasant loop around the Great Langdale and back into Ambleside on quiet roads or a longer route out around Coniston Water that can be easily split over two days.

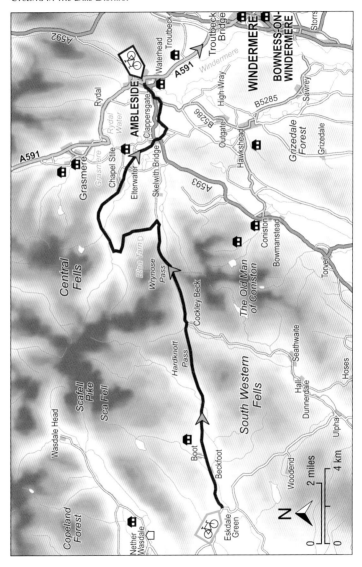

STAGE 5A

Eskdale Green to Ambleside over the passes

Start	Eskdale Green (SD 142 002)
Finish	Ambleside (NY 377 045)
Distance	35km (22 miles)
Climb	830m
Grade	Short/challenging
Time	5–6hrs
OS maps	89, 90
Cafés/pubs	Eskdale Green, Boot, Langdale Chapel Stile, Skelwith Bridge, Ambleside
Maximum gradient	33%
Major climbs	Hardknott Pass: 2.2km, 298m, 33%; Wrynose Pass: 2.5km, 278m, 18%

This route starts with a few undulating miles easing you into the ride before climbing two passes that will be the climax of any tour designed to be challenging. But rather than heading directly to the end, there is a pleasant detour through the Central Fells to give you some easy riding while basking in your achievement.

From Eskdale Green take the left turn at the King George IV Inn towards Langdale and **Hardknott Pass**. ▶ The 7km of easy riding through boot to the foot of the climb gives ample time to warm up, but then it begins in earnest. The good news is the ascent is only 2.2km; the bad news is that it is said to be the steepest road in England and goes to a height of 393m.

> If you need someone to curse, blame the **Romans** who built a road called the Tenth Highway over the pass during the second century to link their coastal fort at Ravenglass with their garrisons at Ambleside and Kendal. Once they abandoned Britain around AD400, the road fell into disrepair and became little

It is perhaps early for a stop, but who can resist having their photograph taken next to a sign warning of a 30 per cent gradient ahead.

*Ascending
Hardknott Pass*

more than a packhorse route, which was destroyed by tanks training on the pass during World War II. After the war a new road was built alongside the original Roman road giving a motor route between Ambleside and Eskdale for the first time.

Like most hills, it is not uniformly steep; it starts off at a gradient of about 20 per cent, eases off into single figures in the middle, then finishes with some snaking hairpins and gradients of 30 per cent and over. The effort of looking up is rewarded with stunning scenery.

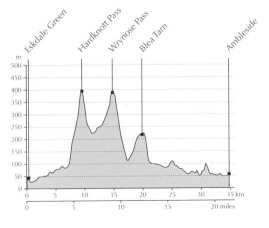

Test your brakes and gingerly set off on the descent, which starts gently enough but soon becomes just as twisty and steep as the ascent. The road through **Cockley Beck** gives some time to recover before climbing over **Wrynose Pass**. It is a far gentler ascent than its neighbour and starts with a 2km stretch through Wrynose Bottom where gradients never get into double figures. But as the sides of the valley begin to close in and there is nowhere to go but up, it culminates in 500m of hard pedalling where gradients are well over 15 per cent. ▶

The descent will be over in a flash, but do not go too fast because just before Little Langdale, the route turns sharply left to Great Langdale. The road climbs up around the western flank of Lingmoor Fell before dropping down into Great Langdale. From now on it is easy riding all the way to the finish. Ride through **Chapel Stile** and down to **Skelwith Bridge** to meet the A593. Rather than following the main road to the finish, turn right across the River Brathay and immediately left into a narrow lane following National Cycle Route 37. This will lead you through Skelwith Fold to re-join the A593 at **Clappersgate**, leaving only a short stretch of main road to ride before the end in **Ambleside**.

The Three Shire Stone at the top of Wrynose Pass was erected in 1860 to mark the location where the historic counties of Lancashire, Cumberland and Westmorland met.

Road block in Little Langdale on a frosty morning

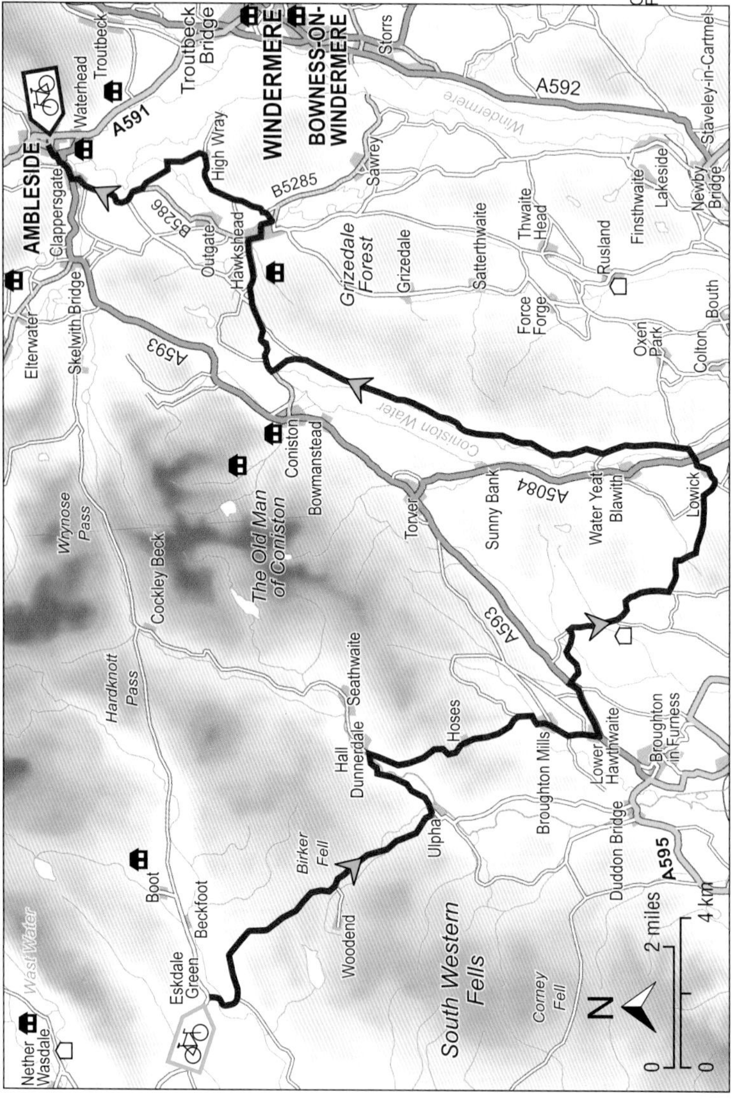

AMBLESIDE
Waterhead
Troutbeck
Troutbeck Bridge
WINDERMERE
BOWNESS-ON-WINDERMERE
Storrs
Cartmel Fell
A591
A592
Windermere
Staveley-in-Cartmel
Clappersgate
High Wray
B5285
B5286
Sawrey
Outgate
Hawkshead
Grizedale Forest
Grizedale
Satterthwaite
Thwaite Head
Rusland
Finsthwaite
Lakeside
Newby Bridge
Elterwater
Skelwith Bridge
A593
Force Forge
Oxen Park
Colton
Bouth
Coniston Water
Coniston
Bowmanstead
The Old Man of Coniston
Torver
Sunny Bank
A5084
Water Yeat
Blawith
Lowick
Wrynose Pass
Cockley Beck
Hardknott Pass
Seathwaite
Hall Dunnerdale
Hoses
Broughton Mills
Lower Hawthwaite
Broughton in Furness
Duddon Bridge
A595
Ulpha
Birker Fell
Woodend
Boot
Beckfoot
Eskdale Green
Wast Water
Nether Wasdale
South Western Fells
Corney Fell
N
0
2 miles
0
4 km

STAGE 5B

Eskdale Green to Ambleside via
Coniston and Hawkshead

Start	Eskdale Green (SD 142 002)
Finish	Ambleside (NY 377 045)
Distance	57km (36 miles)
Climb	1450m
Grade	Long/hard
Time	7–8hrs
OS maps	89, 90, 96
Cafés/pubs	Eskdale Green, Coniston, Hawkshead, Ambleside
Maximum gradient	13%

This is a less challenging but longer route through the South West Fells that could easily be split over two days. After two steady climbs to cross the Duddon Valley, the route follows the quiet back roads beside Coniston Water and through the woods around Hawkshead, with plenty of tourist attractions along the way.

Leave Eskdale Green heading towards Broughton and climb up and over **Birker Fell**. On a clear day, the views northwards towards Scafell Pike and the Western Fells are stunning. Turn left in **Ulpha** and head up the Duddon Valley to **Hall Dunnerdale** and once over the bridge turn right towards Broughton Mills and climb up and over the Dunnerdale Fells. Ride through **Broughton Mills** and turn left on the A593 towards Coniston. After just over a kilometre, turn right towards Woodland and drop sharply downhill through Rosthwaite. At the T junction at the end of this road, turn right towards Ulverston. Then, just after a cattle grid, turn left still heading towards Ulverston and ascend Blawith Knott.

Once over the top, turn left at unsigned junction next to a stone plinth where a local farmer used to leave milk churns for collection in the days before refrigerated tankers. At the end of this gated road, ignore the lane that joins on the left, turning left at an unsigned T junction at the very end and ride through **Lowick** and across the A5084. Immediately after crossing the River Crake at Lowick Bridge, turn left towards Nibthwaite and ride all the way up the east side of **Coniston Water**. ◀

To visit the village turn left at the head of the lake.

CONISTON

When the railway arrived in 1859, it transformed Coniston from a village that served the simple needs of local farming and mining communities into a tourist destination. During the Victorian era, its popularity increased when the poet and social critic John Ruskin (1819–1900) purchased the mansion Brantwood above the eastern shore of Coniston Water in 1871. He championed artists such as JMW Turner and the Pre-Raphaelite School, despite his wife Effie becoming the wife of Edward Millais after their own brief and troubled marriage. His interests and influence spanned art, crafts, conservation, education and politics. He is buried in the churchyard of St Andrews, Coniston and commemorated in the Ruskin Museum, which also covers aspects of local history.

By the time the railway closed in 1962, Coniston was firmly established on the tourist trail, its popularity boosted when the author Arthur Ransome (1884–1967) used the area as a setting in his hugely successful *Swallows and Amazons* series of children's books. The village hit the headlines again in 1967 when Donald Campbell, who broke eight absolute world speed records on water and on land in the 1950s and 1960s, fatally crashed in the rocket powered 'Bluebird'. His body was recovered and buried in the village churchyard in 2001.

At the head of Coniston Water, turn right on the B5285 heading for Hawkshead, and climb up through the woodland and over Hawkshead Hill. Turn right at the T junction with the B5286 and ride into **Hawkshead**.

Hawkshead was an important centre for trading wool in medieval times and later became a market town after being granted a charter by King James I in 1608. By then the town had gained a grammar

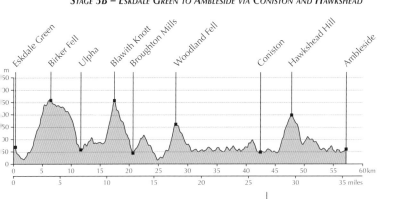

school, which was established by Archbishop Edwin Sandys of York in 1585. Its most famous pupil was the poet William Wordsworth who described its warren of alleys, overhanging gables and medieval squares in his poem, *The Prelude*.

Hawkshead's other famous literary connection is the children's writer and illustrator Beatrix Potter (1866–1944), who purchased Hill Top Farm

Birker Fell against a panorama of higher fells

The rooves of Hawkshead looking towards the Central Fells

in Near Sawrey at the opposite end of Esthwaite Water in 1906. Her husband William Heelis ran his legal practice from the 17th-century building which the National Trust now runs as The Beatrix Potter Gallery.

Leave the village heading south towards Sawrey on the B5285, but once across Black Beck, which feeds into Esthwaite Water hidden away beyond the trees, turn left towards Wray. The roads skirts around slopes of Latterbarrow, through **High Wray** and Low Wray to meet the **B5286** again. Bear right to reach **Clappersgate** and right again to finish in **Ambleside**.

DAY RIDES

Parked up near Hartsop at the bottom of Kirkstone Pass

AMBLESIDE
AND THE CENTRAL LAKES

ROUTE 1

*Over the Wrynose and Hardknott
passes from Ambleside*

Distance	68km (42 miles)
Climb	1580m
Grade	Long/challenging
Time	6–7hrs
OS maps	90, 96
Cafés/pubs	Ambleside, Little Langdale, Boot, Eskdale Green, Broughton Mills, Torver, Coniston
Start and finish	Ambleside (NY 377 045)
Maximum gradient	30%
Major climbs	Wrynose Pass: 2.9km, 280m, 25%; Hardknott Pass: 1.8km, 180m, 30%

After a few miles to get warmed up, there are two big climbs that come in rapid succession and two lesser climbs after the turn for home making this route a must for those wanting to put their climbing ability to the test.

A road sign here warns of the hazards and steep gradients of the Wrynose and Hardknott passes, making an ideal stop for a photograph.

Leave Ambleside and head west on the A593 towards Coniston. Shortly after crossing **Skelwith Bridge**, turn right towards Elterwater. At the bottom of the hill, turn left towards Little Langdale. ◄ After a gentle climb up through Little Langdale village, there is a pleasant descent past Little Langdale Tarn.

Keep left at the cattle grid. Once past the Grade II listed Fell Foot Farm, which was one of the 16 farms that Beatrix Potter left to the National Trust, the road starts to climb. It is fairly easy to start with, but once past Hollin

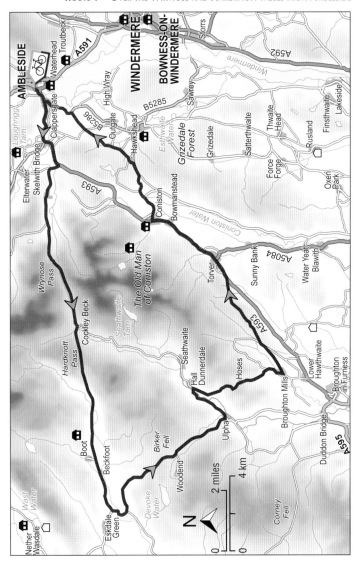

Another of the properties that Beatrix Potter left to the National Trust. Fell Foot Farm is the last dwelling before the start of Wrynose Pass.

During the depression of the 1930s, Beatrix Potter encouraged her tenants to offer B&B and those at Fell Foot Farm, which she left to the National Trust, still do.

Crag, where the full extent of **Wrynose Pass** becomes visible for the first time, the gradient increases and never eases until the summit. ◄

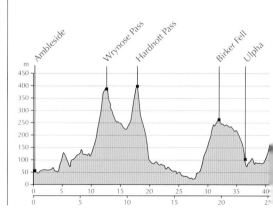

Once past Three Shires Stone at the summit, the initial part of the descent is steep and twisting and needs care, but the long run out through Wrynose Bottom is pure pleasure. Cross the packhorse bridge that spans the River Duddon at **Cockley Beck** and set out up **Hardknott Pass**. It is neither a long climb, nor a high climb. And nowhere does it reach the lung bursting gradients that are experienced when climbing it from the Eskdale side. However, a quick look at an Ordnance Survey map shows seven gradient markers

Heading off up Wrynose Pass with the Langdale Pikes on the skyline

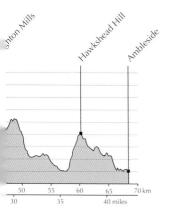

115

EVERESTING ON HARDKNOTT PASS

'Everesting' – repeatedly climbing the same hill until 8848m of ascent has been achieved – is an increasingly popular cycling challenge. Doing it on the gradients of Hardknott Pass would be punishing as you would need to climb Hardknott Pass 30 times from west to east or 50 times east to west to complete an 'Everest'.

However, it would be very appropriate: the passenger in the first car to cross both the Hardknott and Wrynose passes in 1923 was Andrew 'Sandy' Irvine (1902–1922), who was last seen alive making for the summit of Everest with George Mallory on 8 June the following year. The driver was the wealthy motoring fanatic Dick Summers who Irvine had first met at Shrewsbury School. At the time Summers was courting Irvine's sister, Elizabeth, who he eventually married in 1925, while the 21-year-old Sandy was having an affair with Summers' 25-year-old step mother. Neither was said to be happy about the other's relationship, which may have created a tense atmosphere for the other passengers in the open-topped Vauxhall 30-98, the Keswick rock climber and photographer, George Abraham, and his two young daughters.

clustered in less than 500m half way up. It is this stretch that makes many riders consider it to be the hardest ascent in the Lake District, especially the straight 30 per cent ramp near the beginning. Here, any lack of commitment means stalling and then walking until the gradient eases and it is possible to get going again. After that there are several hairpins where, unless there are any vehicles, it is possible to minimise the gradient by going wide.

There are three parts to the descent with two steeper sections that need care sandwiching a more benign middle section. Not that it matters much when going downhill. Other than for a short ascent at Dalegarth, the road through Eskdale is also gently downhill, giving some marvellous riding through **Boot** and all the way to the T junction near the King George IV Inn on the outskirts of **Eskdale Green**.

Turn left towards Broughton and a long climb up and over **Birker Fell**. This is not a single peak as its name suggests, but a high moor with numerous crags rising above

the undulating terrain. Once in **Ulpha**, turn left up the Duddon Valley towards Seathwaite and enjoy a couple of easy kilometres to **Hall Dunnerdale**. Once across the River Duddon, turn right towards **Broughton Mills** and climb up and over the Dunnerdale Fells. It is a short sharp ascent with gradients on the lower section through Far Kiln Bank reaching into the low teens. But once over the top there is the well-earned reward of another long descent. After crossing the River Lickle, turn left towards Torver and climb up and over the lower slopes to Broughton Moor to reach the A593.

Passing through Hall Dunnderdale in the Duddon Valley

Turn left and ride through **Torver** to Coniston, enjoying the views out across Coniston Water. You could ride all the way back to Ambleside on the main road, but a quieter option is to turn right towards Hawkshead in the centre of the village and follow the B5285 around the head of **Coniston Water** and up Hawkshead Hill to the aptly named High Cross. Turn left towards Ambleside and ride through Barnsgates to meet the **B5286** at Pull Woods. Turn left and enjoy the last few miles down to meet the A593 at **Clappersgate**. Turn right to return to **Ambleside**.

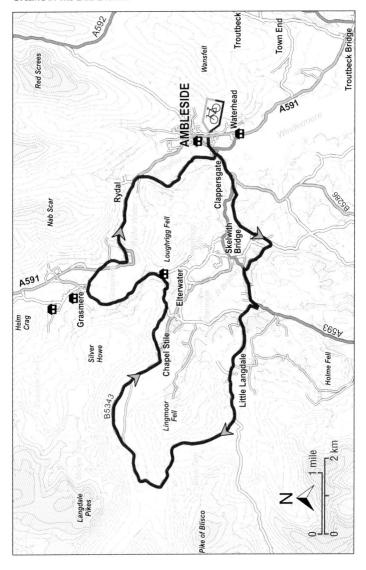

ROUTE 2

Around the Central Fells

Distance	31km (19 miles)
Climb	506m
Grade	Short/moderate
Time	2–3hrs
OS maps	90
Cafés/pubs	Ambleside, Little Langdale, Great Langdale, Chapel Stile, Grasmere, Rydal
Start and finish	Ambleside (NY 377 045)
Maximum gradient	11%

Many would say the compact Central Fells contain the very best of everything that the Lake District has to offer with the dramatic Langdale Pikes and the pretty villages of Grasmere and Rydal where the poet William Wordsworth (1770–1850) lived for half a century. Consequently it is also the busiest, but this route sticks to the quieter lanes away from the main roads wherever possible.

Leave Ambleside and head west on the A593 towards Coniston. Turn left in **Clappersgate** to cross the River Rothay, then immediately right and follow National Cycle Route 37 to Skelwith Fold. Bear left in the centre of the village towards Hawkshead and climb uphill for 500 metres before turning right into an unmarked lane. The climbing continues up and around the northern slopes of Park Fell, but it is well worth it as there are excellent views across to the Langdale Pikes. The lane drops sharply down to meet the busy A593. Turn left to Coniston and follow the main road for 1km, then turn right towards Elterwater. At the bottom of the hill, turn left towards Little Langdale.

A road sign here warns of the hazards and steep gradients of the Wrynose and Hardknott passes, but there

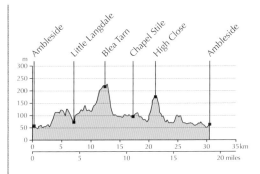

On a clear day, the views gradually unfold revealing a classic Lakeland panorama with Crinkle Crags and Bowfell to the left of Rossett Gill and the Langdale Pikes to the right.

is nothing as arduous on this route. A gentle climb leads up to **Little Langdale** village before a pleasant descent down past Little Langdale Tarn with views opening out in all directions. Immediately after the cattle grid, bear right towards Great Langdale and climb around the flank of Lingmoor Fell through a patch of holly and juniper bushes and past the lonely Blea Tarn before a well-earned descent down into Great Langdale. ◀ From the second cattle grid there is no more pedalling required

Hillside farm near Little Langdale

120

until The Old Dungeon Ghyll Hotel, where the Hikers Bar may be irresistible.

> Those hostelling could raise a glass at **The Old Dungeon Ghyll** to the memory of the wealthy historian Professor GM Trevelyan (1876–1962). In 1929, at the age of 53, he used money left to him by his father to purchase the hotel and then immediately gifted it to the National Trust. The following year he became the founding president of the British Youth Hostel Association.
>
> If you need a reason for a second round, you could toast Geoffrey Winthrop Young (1876–1958), the pioneering rock climber, who became Trevelyan's lifelong friend after meeting at Trinity College, Cambridge in the 1890s. Winthrop Young was instrumental in setting up the Duke of Edinburgh Award Scheme, the Outward Bound movement and the British Mountaineering Council.

Other than for traffic, it is easy cycling all the way down the Langdale Valley. Just at the start of **Chapel**

Heading towards Chapel Stile in the Langdale Valley

Stile, turn left towards the church up an unsigned road that warns of width restrictions. This leads up behind the village, past Langdale YHA and down into popular **Grasmere**.

Look for signs to Ambleside and leave Grasmere following the B5287 past the village church and over the River Rothay to meet the A591. Turn right towards Ambleside at the mini-roundabout then immediately left into Townend, a narrow lane alongside the buildings of the Wordsworth Trust. ◀ The lane passes Dove Cottage, where Wordsworth first lived in Grasmere, then climbs up around White Moss Common to give views down over Grasmere, but soon ends back at the main A591. Turn left and ride around **Rydal Water** and past Rydal Hall, a 16th-century mansion built for the Le Fleming family with a main front dating from the early 19th century, before turning right towards Under Loughrigg. Once across Pelter Bridge, a fine little packhorse bridge that is Grade II listed, keep left and follow the **River Rothay** down to meet the A593 at **Clappersgate**. Turn left to the finish in **Ambleside**.

Most of the known drafts of the famous poet's verse are kept here, along with a diverse collection of other manuscripts.

ROUTE 3

A circuit of the Eastern Fells from Ambleside

Distance	66km (41 miles)
Climb	1346m
Grade	Long/hard
Time	5–6hrs
OS maps	90
Cafés/pubs	Ambleside, Kirkstone Pass, Patterdale, Glenridding, Dockray, Troutbeck, Scales, Threlkeld, Grasmere
Start and finish	Ambleside YHA (NY 377 031)
Maximum gradient	25%
Major climbs	The Struggle: 4.5km, 403m, 20%

When a road is called 'The Struggle' you know it is going to require some effort and that is certainly true of this iconic Lakeland ascent. But once at the top of Kirkstone Pass, the rest of the ride is fairly relaxing and loops around the north of the Helvellyn range before returning through St John's in the Vale, Thirlmere and Grasmere.

As the hardest part of this route comes early on, it makes good sense to ride a couple of miles on the flat to get warmed up. If you are setting out from Ambleside YHA you will get this anyway.

The steep climb out of Ambleside at the start of 'The Struggle'

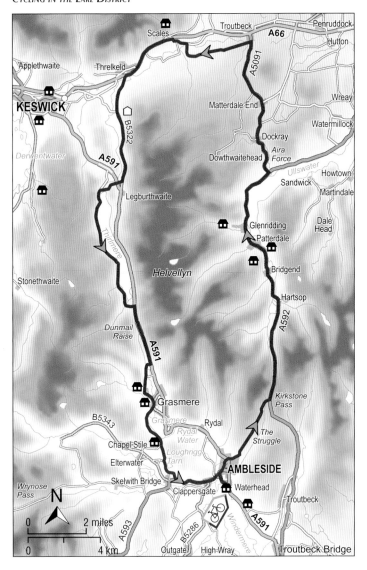

Bridge House in Ambleside; once an apple store, now a tourist information centre

Head north through the town following the A591 towards Keswick until you reach a mini-roundabout on Rydal Road. Turn sharply right following the signs for Kirkstone up the narrow and brutally steep Smithy Brow and onwards up Kirkstone Road. It's obvious why this road is called The Struggle but it is pleasant riding between tidy dry stone walls below an occasional canopy of trees. But as you climb, the trees get scrubbier and the stone walls less well tended. A flat section at after about 4km gives a welcome respite before the final short, sharp push to the summit. If visibility is poor, the sudden appearance of double yellow lines either side of the road warn of the approaching junction. ▶

The 18th-century Bridge House was originally the store for Old Ambleside Hall built across Stock Beck to save on land tax.

Crossing the dam at Thirlmere

Turn left on to the A592 towards Patterdale and Penrith and follow the smooth, fast road to Ullswater. After a few kilometres of undulating riding along the northern shore of **Ullswater**, turn left on to the A5091 towards Dockray. The road climbs gently with Glencoyne Park on the left and the ravine of Aira Beck with the 20m Aira Force waterfall below you on the right.

The hotel at **Dockray** is the final opportunity for refreshments before the road climbs steadily up through the tiny hamlet of **Matterdale End** and across the open hillside around the squat cone of Great Mell Fell. Then, once clear of the conifer plantation, easy riding resumes. Just to the south of

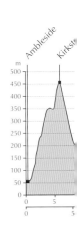

Troutbeck, take the small road signposted for Gill Head Campsite and follow it all the way to Wallthwaite where it turns north between two farms to join another stretch of road that runs parallel to the main road A66. ▶

Turn left and ride westwards to meet the A66. Cross the main road and follow the cycle path westwards towards Keswick. For a brief while this C2C path follows a loop of the old road in front of the White Horse Inn and Bunkhouse only to return to run alongside the road for another 2km before branching off between the trees and out on to a gated road to **Threlkeld**, where there is an excellent café behind the village hall.

After the Threlkeld Public Rooms, turn left into Station Road, cross the A66 and take the B5322 towards Thirlmere. The road meanders pleasantly through St John's in the Vale sandwiched between the rocky slopes of Clough Head on one side and St John's Beck on the other. Just before the junction with the A591, turn right following a short stretch of gravelled cycle path towards Grasmere, then cross the A591 still following the cycle path to cross the dam at the head of **Thirlmere** and pick up the shore road. ▶

On a clear day, there is a fine panorama of Blencathra with the serrated ridge of Sharp Edge clearly visible on its eastern flank.

Thirlmere was built in the 1890s to supply water to Manchester through 96 miles of aqueducts and pipes with a drop of 20in along every mile of its length.

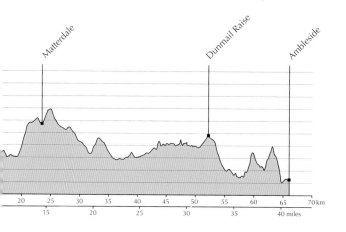

Helvellyn, the third highest Lakeland summit, from the shore of Thirlmere

At the southern end of Thirlmere, turn right on to the A591 towards Ambleside climbing up and over **Dunmail Raise**. Turn right on to the minor road at Town Head and drop sharply down through a farmyard. The road crosses the River Rothay, but rather than cross it again turn right just before the next bridge otherwise you will end up back on the main road. Turn left at the T junction at the end of this road and ride into **Grasmere**. Turn right at the village green into Broadgate and right again at the end into Red Bank Road. Follow this all the way around the west side of Grasmere to **Elterwater**, through High Close and onwards past **Loughrigg Tarn** to meet the A593. Turn left to return to the start in **Ambleside**.

GRASMERE

Ironically the poet William Wordsworth's dread of having his beloved Lake District overrun with tourists has come home to roost with a vengeance in his own adopted home of Grasmere. He first moved into Dove Cottage with his sister Dorothy in 1799, but after he married his childhood friend Mary Hutchinson in 1802, the growing family needed more space and moved around the village. They first went to Allan Bank in 1808, then to the Old Rectory in 1810 and finally to Rydal Mount in 1813. Today, Dove Cottage is owned by The Wordsworth Trust; Rydal Mount by the poet's descendants and Allan Bank by the National Trust, while the Old Rectory, where the youngest two of his five children died, remains a private residence. Wordsworth died while out walking in 1850 and is buried alongside his wife Mary, who died nine years later, with a simple tombstone in the churchyard of St Oswald's Church. Their grave is now one of the most visited literary shrines in the world.

It isn't only Wordsworth that attract the crowds: there are many gift shops and places to stay and eat, and it is done in the very best of taste with little touches such as the recently created Wordsworth Daffodil Garden where you can own a share and have an engraved stone set in the path to mark your benevolence.

Autumn colours at Grasmere

PENRITH
AND THE NORTH EAST

ROUTE 4
Haweswater and Ullswater from Shap

Distance	68km (42 miles); extension 81km (50 miles)
Climb	888m
Grade	Medium/hard
Time	5–6hrs; extension 5½–6½hrs
OS maps	90, 91
Cafés/pubs	Shap, Bampton, Helton, Askham, Pooley Bridge, Tirril, Yanwath
Start and finish	Car park, Main Street, Shap NY 564 149
Maximum gradient	8%

Its easy access makes Shap an ideal place to start this ride that visits both Haweswater Reservoir and Ullswater before returning to the start through the peaceful villages on the other side of the motorway.

Henry VIII closed the 12th-century Shap Abbey in 1540 and the stone was incorporated into later buildings such as Lowther Castle. All that remains is an impressive 15th-century tower.

◄ At the top of the village, turn left towards Haweswater, then left into **Rosgill**, crossing the River Lowther where dippers can occasionally be seen walking along the river bed. Turn left through the hamlet of Bomby, left at the junction on the other side and then left again at the next crossroad, which goes all the way to Haweswater.

Extension to Mardale Common

It is 6.5km down the eastern side of the reservoir to the road end at Mardale Common – and 6.5km back, but it is well worth it as it is gloriously wild and empty. The waterside road is also regular and flat, so it takes no time at all, 30mins at most.

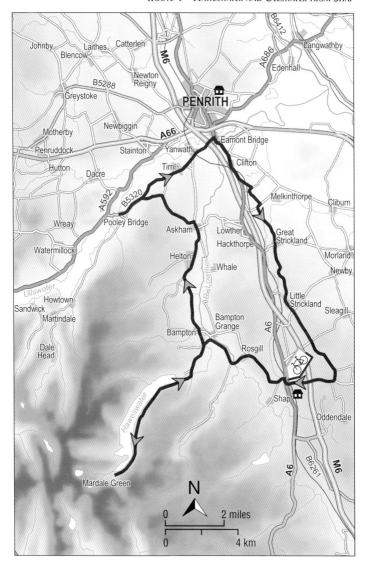

VILLAGES LOST AND VILLAGES REGAINED

In particularly dry summers, the receding waters of Haweswater reveal the ghostly remains of the former farming village Mardale Green above the muddy floor of the reservoir. It and the neighbouring village of Measand were evacuated in 1935 after Parliament allowed Manchester Corporation to flood the valley to provide much needed water for the towns and cities of the North West. Up until then Haweswater had been a 4km-long natural lake, but the dam raised the water level an additional 30m adding another couple of kilometres to its length.

The houses and the centuries-old Dun Bull Inn were demolished, but the village church was systematically dismantled and the stone used in the construction of the dam. The bodies in the churchyard were exhumed and reinterred in Shap churchyard. But what goes around comes around, as the saying goes and as villages were being drowned in front of the dam, a new one sprung up behind it. Prefabricated houses made from concrete and cast iron were erected to provide accommodation for those working on the dam, creating the new settlement of Burnbanks. After construction was complete, the population of the village fell as men were called up for service in World War II and others moved away to other work. Many properties fell to ruin. However, in recent years, this 'pop-up' village has been redeveloped and new houses built so once again there is a community in Haweswater.

Villages are not the only loss to the area. From 1969 until 2003, Golden Eagles nested in the Haweswater Valley, but since the disappearance of the female in 2004, the solitary male has yet to attract a new mate.

Turn left to visit Pooley Bridge and Ullswater, a detour of just 3km and then return the same way following signs for Penrith.

Follow signs for Penrith, turning left in **Bampton** and then riding through **Helton** to **Askham**. Just beyond the village, turn left into a narrow road and ride through Celleron to the junction with the B5230. ◄ The route follows the **B5230** through **Tirril** and **Yanwath** and over the **M6 motorway** to its end at a T junction with the A6 in **Eamont Bridge**. Turn right towards Shap, cross the River Lowther, and then turn left towards Brougham Hall and Brougham Castle.

At the crossroads just to the south of Brougham Castle, follow the weight-limited C3074 southwards. Although there is no sign until the next junction, this is National Cycle Route 71 and we stick with it for the next 8km. At the next few junctions, follow it left towards Cliburn, right towards **Clifton** and then through two complex junctions where again there are no way-marks. Just stay to the east of the railway line and keep heading

Riding up through Askham considered by many to be one of the prettiest villages in Cumbria

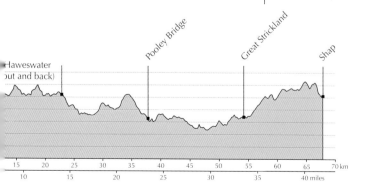

133

Brougham Castle on the bank of the River Eamont dates from the 13th century

BROUGHAM

Being at the confluence of the rivers Eamont and Lowther made Brougham an important defensive position and the Romans built a fort here call Brocavum. Brougham Hall, in the centre of the village, was built as a fort in the 14th century by the de Burgham family, who are thought to give their name to the village. By the 16th century, the site was transformed with the addition of a manor house and other outbuildings and the 17th century saw the addition of a pele tower. That line of the Broughams died out in 1608 and the Hall was eventually acquired for £1500 in 1651 by the notorious Lady Anne Clifford (1590–1676) who controlled 14 castles in the North West including nearby Brougham Castle. She carried out extensive renovations to the Hall and upon her death left it to her agent James Bird, who oversaw the greatest expansion of work at the Hall.

A distant branch of the original Brougham family re-acquired the hall in 1726 and remodelled it twice in the 19th century. It reached its zenith in late Victorian times when it became known as 'the Windsor of the North' owing to frequent visits from the royal family. The Broughams and the Hall parted ways yet again in 1934 and it rapidly fell into decay. In 1985 it was rescued from dereliction and today it is one of the largest country house restoration projects in England, providing a home to an array of arts and craft workshops and a café.

Brougham Castle, to the east of the village near the original Roman fort, started life as a stone keep surrounded by an earthen bank and a wooden palisade. It was built during the 13th century by the local de Vieuxpont family, who also owned castles at Appelby and Brough. However, in 1269 their estates passed to the Clifford family through marriage adding to their own growing collection of castles in the North West. The castle remained part of the Clifford estate for four

The 12th century door knocker at Brougham Hall which is almost identical to that of Durham Cathedral – both now replaced with replicas

centuries, but with a surfeit of residences to choose from, it went through periods of neglect. In 1643, Lady Anne Clifford inherited the castle and restored it, but after her death at Brougham in 1676, it once again fell into disrepair and the empty shell was left to decay. Today the ruins are conserved by English Heritage.

south. At the next T junction, the blue way-mark signs return and we follow them right and then left to **Great Strickland** where we part company with NR71 and continue south to **Little Strickland**. ▶ Unless you fancy riding the final few kilometres on the busy A6, ignore signs for Shap at the next two crossroads and go straight over at both heading towards Sleagill at the first and Crosby Ravensworth at the second. Turn right towards Shap at both of the next T junctions, going over the **M6 motorway** and the west coast mainline railway to return to the start.

Strickland gets its name from the Old Norse word 'stercaland' meaning pasture, indicating who once dominated these lands and how they farmed them.

ROUTE 5

Lowther Park and Ullswater from Penrith

Distance	57km (36 miles)
Climb	575m
Grade	Medium/moderate
Time	4–5hrs
OS maps	90, 91
Cafés/pubs	Penrith, Carleton, Great Strickland, Hackthorpe, Askham, Pooley Bridge, Wreay, Greystoke, Little Blencow, Newton Reigny
Start and finish	Market Square, Penrith (NY 514 304)
Maximum gradient	6%

A pleasant ride along quiet lanes with the option of using the historic Ullswater Steamers for the 25-minute crossing from Howtown to Pooley Bridge.

Park at one of the many Pay and Display car parks in Penrith and head south from the town centre following signs for the A6 South. Turn left into Roper Street, which quickly becomes Carleton Road and part of National Cycle Route 71. Use the lights to cross the A686 and ride

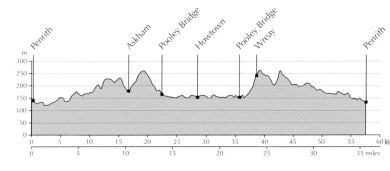

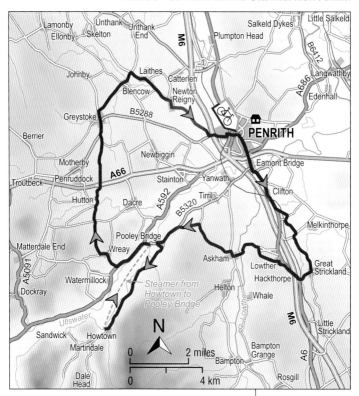

down the road to the right of The Cross Keys. This ends in a cycle path that goes under the busy A66 and over the River Eamont to bring you out near Brougham Castle. Go straight ahead at the crossroads just to the south of the castle, following the NCR71 southwards along the weight-limited C3074.

The route sticks with the NCR71 for a while, turning turn left towards Cliburn at the next junction then right towards **Clifton** shortly afterwards. At the end of this road, turn left in front of Fellview Cottages and quickly left again. At the next T junction, the blue way-mark signs for the

Designed as a single entity from a sketch by the Georgian architect Robert Adam, Lowther Model Village was built in the 1770s to provide accommodation for estate workers.

NCR71 return and we follow them right and then left into **Great Strickland**, where the route leaves the NCR71.

Turn right in the centre of the village towards Lowther, going under the main west coast railway line to meet the A6. Turn right towards Hackthorpe and pass over the **M6 motorway**. Turn left in **Hackthorpe** and follow the road through **Lowther village** and past the Birds of Prey Centre and the visitor entrance to Lowther Castle. ◄

Turn left on a bend towards Askham and left over a cattle grid at the next T junction still following signs for Askham. This is pleasant riding through parkland with the

The western façade of Lowther Castle from the courtyard

ruins of Lowther Castle through the trees on your left. The road passes Lowther parish church with its ostentatious Lonsdale Mausoleum then drops down sharply to cross the **River Lowther**. Local tradition has it that throwing a coin on to a boulder that lies just below the water level beneath Lowther Bridge brings the thrower good luck. Askham parish church is much more modest than its neighbour back

LOWTHER CASTLE

The grey, roofless castle may not look very grand today, but when it was at its most splendid in the 19th and early 20th centuries, it was said to be possible to walk right across Cumbria on land owned by the Lowthers. The family has its roots back in the Dark Ages but came into prominence in the 18th century after 1st Earl of Lonsdale, or 'Wicked Jimmy' as he was known, got in on the boom in iron and coal, acquiring so much land that the estate became the largest in England. He had inherited the Lowther estate from a cousin and another fortune from his father, who was the Governor of Barbados. But these were nothing compared with what he inherited from another cousin, Sir James Lowther of Whitehaven, who left to him that town, its harbour and trade, coal mines, minerals and two million pounds, which amounted to about a quarter of the annual British exports at that time. He used his wealth to monopolise iron-ore extraction in Cumberland and to control the nine parliamentary boroughs in the North West.

His success secured the families fortunes for the next century. After his death in 1802, his distant cousin William inherited the estate and built Lowther Castle. Expansion into railways in the Victorian era further increased the family fortunes. But by the beginning of the 20th century, the Cumbrian coal and iron mining industries were in decline and no longer generating the wealth needed to support the extravagant lifestyles of subsequent earls or to pay crippling death duties after their passing. The castle was vacated in 1936 and the roof removed in 1957 to reduce the burden of rates. In recent decades, the family has focussed on developing the land assets of the Lowther Estate, occasionally supplementing their income by disposing of assets such as oil paintings and the iconic northern fell Blencathra.

In 2010 the castle and gardens were leased to an independent trust and since then charitable funding has allowed the castle and its gardens to be developed into a major visitor attraction with a café and shop in the stable courtyard.

Riding down the zig-zags at Martindale with Howtown below

From Howtown it's only 3.5km to the road ends at Dale Head and Boredale Head including a snaking climb up The Hause that gives tremendous views along Ullswater.

up the hill, but the village of **Askham** is a delight with solid stone houses set around two village greens.

Turn right towards Penrith, then just beyond the village, turn left towards Celleron along a narrow lane that gives good views back to Lowther Castle and out to Dacre Castle just to the north of Ullswater. Turn left at the junction with the **B5230** towards Pooley Bridge and left again within sight of the village to follow the road down the eastern shore of **Ullswater** to **Howtown** and take a boat to Pooley Bridge. ◄

Boats have been providing excursions around Ullswater for more than 150 years. Today there is a fleet of five boats including the 'MY Lady of the Lake', which was launched in 1877 and is believed to be the oldest working passenger vessel in the world. They all have fully licensed bars and provide teas, coffees and light refreshments. There are nine sailings a day during the summer months but only two in winter. Bikes are stored in racks and currently the fare for crossing from Howtown to Pooley

Bridge for rider and bike will give you sufficient change from £10 for a cup of tea.

Disembark, cross the River Eamont and continue around to the A592 down the western side of the lake. Turn right at the Brackenrigg Inn and ride up to Bennethead, then right again towards Greystoke. Just before crossing Dacre Beck, we pick up the NCR71 and follow it through Hutton John to the A66. Dismount and cross using the safe areas between the carriageways, then continue northwards on NCR71, joining the B5288 for the final stretch into **Greystoke**. ▸ Stay with NCR71 for another 3km until a staggered crossroads just beyond **Blencow**. Turn right towards Penrith and follow NCR7 through **Laithes** and **Newton Reigny**, where Catterlen Hall – a large house constructed around a 15th-century pele tower – can be glimpsed from the road. Follow NCR7 through Newton Rigg campus, under the M6 motorway and main west coast railway to emerge in Thacka Lane. Turn right and ride back to the start in the centre of **Penrith**.

Greystoke Cycle Café is neither metropolitan nor staffed by moody baristas, but it is on the route just to the north of the village and is well worth stopping off for.

MV Lady Wakefield awaiting passengers at Pooley Bridge

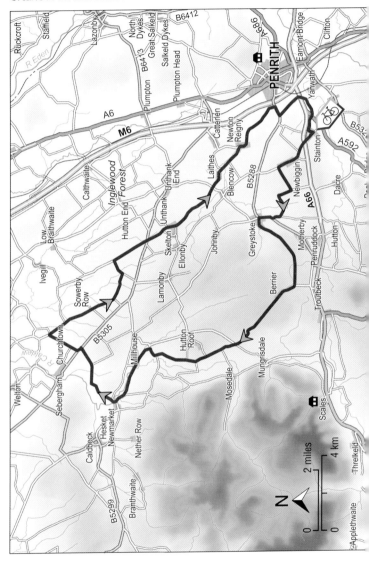

ROUTE 6
Around Inglewood Forest

Distance	56km (35 miles)
Climb	555m
Grade	Medium/moderate
Time	3–4hrs
OS maps	90
Cafés/pubs	Stainton, Newbiggin, Greystoke, Hesket Newmarket, Sour Nook, Skelton, Little Blencow, Rheged
Start and finish	St Johns Road, Stainton (NY 486 284)
Maximum gradient	6%

Although it only briefly slips within the boundaries of the national park, this day ride is an enjoyable one through some delightful Cumbrian villages in the Inglewood Forest, an area that was set aside after the Norman Conquest for hunting deer and wild boar. Today the largest remaining area of forest is used for motor rallying.

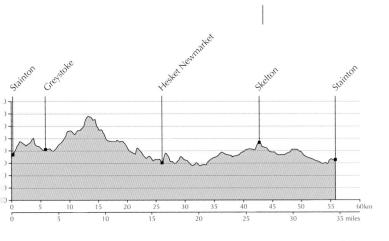

*The welcoming
Greystoke Cycle
Café on the road
to Blencow*

Park considerably in Stainton. Then head north at the crossroads in the centre of the village along The Pavilion towards Greenriggs passing under the busy **A66** to pick up a variant of the C2C cycle path. Follow this along the north side of the main road and all the way to **Newbiggin**. Ride through the village centre, which was once a busy centre for quarrying limestone, then turn left towards CCC Flusco; the county council's house-hold waste recycling depot, which is hidden away in one of the disused quarries. Just after the caravan site, turn right on a bend towards Greystoke. Shortly after Greystoke Gill, turn right on to a road that is part of the C2C cycle route, and ride into **Greystoke** joining the B5288 for the last few hundred metres.

There has been a fortification at **Greystoke** since just after the Norman Conquest in 1066, but the present castle, which is a private house, dates from the mid-Victorian era when the Howard family who have lived there since the 16th century rebuilt it. The author Edgar Rice Burroughs (1875–1950) gave his hero Tarzan, the imaginary title of Lord Greystoke, in his first book *Tarzan of the Apes* in 1912 after making friends with a member of the Howard family during the second Boer War (1899–1902), which he reported on as a war correspondent.

The castle is screened behind plantations and high stone walls, but the garden of the Greystoke Cycle Café provides a sneaky view of it across the parkland.

Turn left at the broad village green towards Berrier. At the end of this road, turn right towards Hutton Roof and follow this long straight road through **Berrier** and onwards for the next 10km, following signs for Millhouse. Soon the River Caldew comes in from the Northern Fells and runs parallel to the road, but at Haltcliffe Bridge, just after the road turns away from the river up a sharp little climb, turn left towards Caldwell and Millhouse, where the route rejoins the river all the way into **Hesket Newmarket**. Take time to ride up into this pretty village, but return to the bottom of the broad main street and follow the road though Newlands and out to the **B5305**.

Hesket Newmarket is famed for its co-operatively-owned pub and brewery

Turn left towards Sebergham then quickly right at the Sour Nook Inn towards Raughton Head.

As the road bends to the north, turn right following National Cycle Route 7 towards Penrith, turning left at Skelton Wood End then right at the next junction towards Skelton. Cross the B5305 and keep following NCR7 through the villages of **Skelton**, **Laithes** and **Newton Reigny**. NCR7 turns left through the campus at Newton Rigg, but this route goes straight on to the end of the road. Turn right towards Greystoke on the B5288, then after 1km, turn left towards Skirsgill, just before the Greystoke Pillar. ◄ At the junction with the A66, use the cycle path to cross both carriageways, and then take the road alongside the hotel through Redhills. The café at Rheged Exhibition and Discovery Centre is an obvious attraction to a weary cyclist in need of cake, but otherwise turning left and then right across the A592 takes you back to **Stainton** where the ride began.

This obelisk was erected by the 11th Duke of Norfolk of Greystoke Castle in the 18th century to mark the southern tip of Inglewood Forest.

KESWICK
AND THE NORTH WEST

ROUTE 7
Loop around the Back o' Skiddaw

Distance	54km (34 miles)
Climb	815m
Grade	Medium/moderate
Time	4–5hrs
OS maps	90
Cafés/pubs	Keswick, Scales, Mungrisdale, Hesket Newmarket, Bassenthwaite, Keswick
Start and finish	Keswick YHA (NY 267 235)
Maximum gradient	9%

This rides does an anti-clockwise circuit of the Northern Fells, first following the C2C cycle trail as far as Scales before heading around the Back o' Skiddaw with Skiddaw, Great Calva and the other fells in the group always on your left.

From Keswick town centre, head up Station Road and across the River Greta towards the museum following the blue way-marker signs that lead to the C2C cycleway (NCR71). Here the trail follows the course of the old Keswick to Penrith railway line so it is gentle pedalling despite steadily gaining height as it weaves its way up alongside the river. Follow the C2C trail through **Threlkeld** and out the other side all the way to **Scales**. Turn left up a gated road alongside the White Horse Inn and follow this around the lower slopes of Souther Fell to its end in **Mungrisdale**, leaving the C2C route at Beckside. ▶

The topology reflects the geological changes below ground, but so too does Southerfell Farm which is built from local granite and slate with sandstone window surrounds from the Eden Valley.

A typical Lakeland farm nestling into the hillside near Scales

Ride on through Bowscale and **Mosedale**. In the middle of Caldbeck Common, turn left, cross Carrock Beck and climb around the eastern flank of Carrock Fell to Calebreck before a pleasant descent into **Hesket Newmarket**. Turn left into the village, up the broad main street, and out the

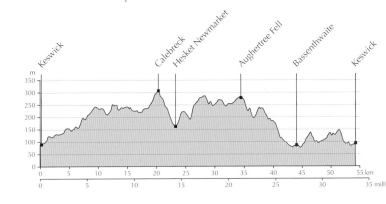

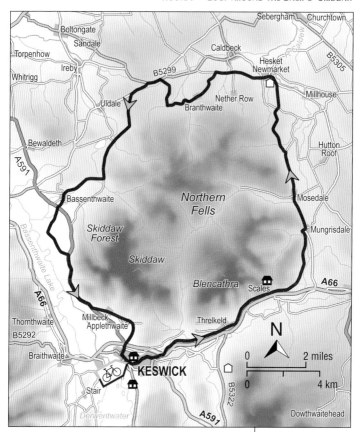

other side following a narrow lane immediately to the left of Berkeley House towards Fellside and Branthwaite. After a short climb, turn left on to a smaller lane, still following signs for Fellside and Branthwaite.

Just after **Branthwaite** this road eventually turns into a track. Avoid that by turning right at a large agricultural shed and heading northwards to a T junction on the **B5299**. Turn left following directions for Keswick, which has clearly been added to this signpost as an afterthought.

Splashing through the ford at Carrock Beck

Near the summit of Aughertree Fell, turn left following signs for Orthwaite and Mirkholme, dropping down to Longlands before skirting around the western slopes of the Uldale Fells with first Chapelhouse Reservoir and then Over Water below on your right. You are now on Regional Cycle Route 38, which you follow all the way to Keswick.

A kilometre south of the village, turn sharply right towards Bassenthwaite, dropping gently down through Park Wood. Turn left across the bridge and ride through **Bassenthwaite**, crossing the green beneath an avenue of trees. Turn left and then right, heading south towards the A591. Cross the main road taking an unsigned lane to the right of Chapel Farm that leads towards Scarness. At the end of this lane, turn left along the northern shore of **Bassenthwaite Lake**, then turn right at the T junction and follow the A591 towards Keswick.

After 3km, turn left on to a minor road that runs along the foot of the fells passing through **Millbeck** and **Applethwaite**. When this road joins the A591 again, turn left, then cross the A66 at the roundabout and ride into **Keswick**.

WH AUDEN – A MINER POET

Had he not become the most important English poet of the 20th century, Wystan Hugh Auden (1907–1973) might easily have become a mining engineer. In the 1920s, his father bought Far Wescoe, a cottage to the west of Threlkeld, as a holiday home. With the remains of lead mines and quarries all around, the teenage WH Auden soon developed a passion for everything to do with mining, building up a substantial library of books on the subject and visiting disused workings around Carrock Fell and further afield in the North Pennines with older brother John.

Their childhood explorations shaped their lives. John became an eminent geologist and Wystan was initially intent on a career in mining before taking up writing. But even then the experiences never left him. His early poems are full of images of lead mining set against a background of fells, becks and wildlife and he continued to use derelict mine buildings as a metaphor for lost belief in many of his works. Although Auden spent much of his adult life in the USA and eventually became an American citizen, he continued to visit Far Wescoe until his widowed father sold it in 1948. He also paid repeated visits to the North Pennines and the churchyard at Mungrisdale where the ashes of both of his parents were scattered.

However, his name will never be listed alongside Wordsworth and others as a Lakes poet as he found his inspiration in the bleak, austere fells east of Penrith rather than the Lake District which in one poem he thought was perhaps 'Another bourgeois invention like the piano?'

ROUTE 8

Whinlatter and Honister passes from Keswick

Distance	46km (29 miles)
Climb	1025m
Grade	Short/challenging
Time	4–5hrs
OS maps	89
Cafés/pubs	Keswick, Braithwaite, Whinlatter, Low Lorton, Loweswater, Buttermere, Honister, Seatoller, Rosthwaite, Lodore
Start and finish	Keswick (NY 272 238)
Maximum gradient	18%
Major climbs	Whinlatter Pass: 3.3km, 231m, 15%; Honister Pass: 2km, 250m, 18%

This is a ride for anyone unsure of their climbing ability as it goes over two of the Lake District's less demanding high passes with plenty of easier miles and fine scenery in between.

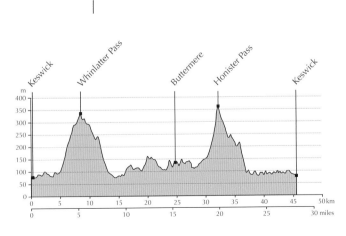

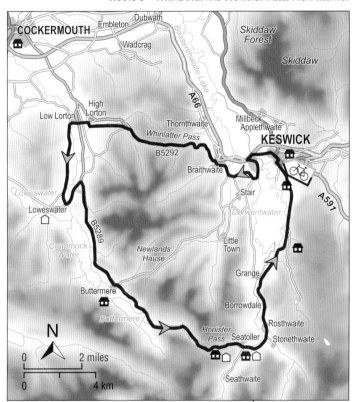

From the centre of Keswick, head up Main Street over the River Greta following road signs for North Cumbria West A66. Once on the outskirts of the town, turn left, following way-marker signs for the C2C cycle trail and cross the bridge over the River Derwent. Keep following the C2C trail through the woods to Ullock and onwards to **Braithwaite**. Ride through the village to meet the **B5292** at the Royal Oak Inn and turn left on to **Whinlatter Pass**. Initially the road climbs gently up the gorse-covered slopes gradually revealing views over Bassenthwaite Lake. But once it turns away from the lake, the climbing

Buttermere Church at the foot of Eskdale Hause

The name Whinlatter is a mix of Old Norse and Gaelic; 'whin' meaning gorse and 'lettir' meaning slope – and there is plenty of both on the way up.

gets harder for a while until the gradient eases off with a long ramp up to the summit. ◀

Having a visitor centre and café at the top of a climb is idyllic as setting off again is painless. After 2km, drop left into a narrow road to pick up the C2C trail again and follow it through **Low Lorton** and across the B5289 towards Thackthwaite. Once over the River Cocker, turn south up the Lorton Valley and ride through Thackthwaite. Turn left at the T junction at the end of the road towards Buttermere and ride through **Loweswater village**, looking out for red squirrels as you climb up Scale Hill. Turn right towards Buttermere at the junction with the B5289.

Once clear of the trees, the view up the valley is magnificent with Grasmoor and Whiteless Pike high on the left and Crummock Water stretched out below. Then once around the headland at Hause Point, the distinctive

THE TEAM TOWNEND PUSHBIKE CHALLENGE

Besides being the brewery tap for Cumbrian Legendary Ales, which were first brewed here in 2003 but are now based in Hawkshead, the 400-year-old Kirkstile Inn at Loweswater is home to the annual Team Townend Pushbike Challenge. The event remembers the lives of brothers Christian and Niggy Townend from Cockermouth, who were killed in a road accident while out cycling in 2010.

Riders are encouraged to get themselves sponsored with all proceeds going to Roadpeace, a charity which supports victims of road traffic collisions and campaigns for much needed improvements in our criminal justice system. The event takes place in April each year with a short course that crosses the Whinlatter and Newlands passes and a longer course that takes in the Honister Pass too. See www.teamtownend.org.

wedge of Fleetwith Pike comes into view in the distance and eventually, after **Buttermere village**, the splendid panorama of the fells above Buttermere: First High Stile opposite the village, then High Crag and finally tucked away in the corner, the rippling buttresses of Haystacks. Given that the last few kilometres have been fairly easy going, it has to be one of the best Lakeland valleys for cycling.

Starting out up Honister Pass

Motor launch on Derwentwater

St Herbert's Island in the middle of the lake is named after an Anglo-Saxon priest and hermit who ate fish from the lake and grew vegetables around his tiny cell.

Now it is time to leave and, as the song goes, the only way is up. Because the valley curves around to the right, the steeper sections of **Honister Pass** remain hidden for some time and the climbing is easy. But once across Gatesgarthdale Beck, the steeper sections at the head of the valley come into view. It still takes some time to reach them and when they come you can gain some consolation in the fact that the gradients only ever get into the high teens and never reach the 25 per cent warned of on the road signs. There is also a very welcome café at the summit too.

Now for the 2.3km descent to Borrowdale. The gradients touch 25 per cent at times so there is little need to pedal and the remainder of the ride back to Keswick is also easy rolling. Once through the Jaws of Borrowdale, where the road twists and turns between rocky cliffs, there are good views up Derwentwater with a backdrop of Skiddaw making an ideal place for one last photograph. Then it's just a few kilometres back to the finish in **Keswick**. ◀

ROUTE 9

Across Allerdale

Distance	60km (37 miles)
Climb	1006m
Grade	Long/hard
Time	5–6hrs
OS maps	85, 89, 90
Cafés/pubs	Cockermouth, Ireby, Caldbeck, Uldale, Kilnhill, Setmurthy
Start and finish	Wordsworth's House, Cockermouth (NY 119 307)
Maximum gradient	9%

This is a pleasant ride in a little visited part of the national park to the north of Bassenthwaite Lake and out to Caldbeck around the Back o' Skiddaw.

From Wordsworth's House, ride east along Main Street, cross over the River Cocker and into Castlegate. At the top, turn left into Isel Road, which quickly becomes a narrow country road alongside the River Derwent. After 5km, turn left over the river and immediately right on the other bank towards Bewaldeth, which sounds as though it should be home to goths and heavy metal fans. But it is a pleasant little hamlet, made all the quieter since the A591 was routed around it with a by-pass. Cross the main road, then after the telephone box turn left through the handful of farms and houses and follow the road around the southern flanks of Binsey. There is no need to climb this little fell to get good views as you can see down to Bassenthwaite Lake and across to the wonderfully named waterfall of Whitewater Dash between Skiddaw and Great Calva from the road. ▶

Hewthwaite Hall at Setmurthy is a fine whitewashed manor house dating from 1581, thought to have been built on the site of an earlier pele tower.

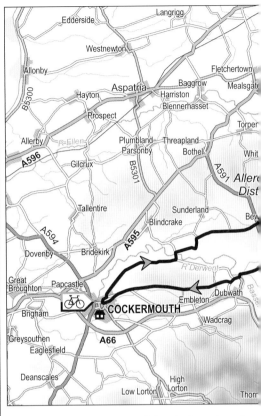

This was once a busy market town but is now an unspoilt, peaceful fell village with only the moot hall and 13th-century butter cross reflecting its busier past.

At the end of the road, turn left and ride northwards through Ruthwaite and downhill to **Ireby**. ◀ Follow signs to Caldbeck at both sets of crossroads in the village, then just beyond the outskirts, turn left towards Sandale. Cross the B5299 at a staggered junction and ride through **Sandale** and over the long western ridge of Seat. There are fine views northwards over the Solway to Scotland on a clear day. The roads in the area run parallel to the streams that drain off the Northern Fells and are straight and level making them ideal for time trialling. But take

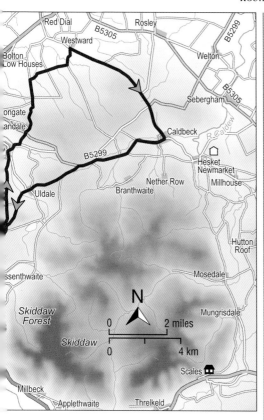

time to look up as you approach the wind turbines and turn right towards Church Hill. This road crosses two of those streams – Pow Gill and Thornthwaite Beck – ending at a T junction. Turn left, still heading towards Church Hill and cross a third stream, Townthwaite Beck. At the crossroads, turn right and ride towards Caldbeck. The road climbs steadily up past the hillside farms of Brocklebank with views across the Eden Valley towards Carlisle. But the last mile after joining the B5299 is a well-earned leisurely downhill into **Caldbeck**.

CALDBECK

Cald Beck, which gives the village its name, provided the water power that turned this quiet corner of the Lake District into a hive of industry from the late 17th century right through to the end of the 19th century with woollen mills, bobbin mills, corn mills, a paper mill and a brewery. Many of the old mill buildings remain.

A short walk that starts at the village duck pond follows the river up the 'Howk', a limestone gorge that contains waterfalls and the picturesque ruins of the old bobbin mill, which was powered by what was said to be the largest waterwheel in the country with a diameter of 42ft. Just below the village church is Priest's Mill, an old watermill which has been restored to full working order and today houses a popular café, shops and workshops.

St Kentigern's churchyard contains a couple of interesting antiquities. The Roughton Stone, which was used to process ores mined in Roughton Gill high above the village in the Caldbeck Fells, commemorates four centuries of mining in the area, right up into the 1960s when the last mine closed. Then there is the grave of the famous huntsman, John Peel (1776–1854) remembered in the 19th-century song 'D'ye ken John Peel'.

He was a rumbustious character, who eloped with the 18-year-old Mary White to marry at Gretna Green, before settling down to a life of hunting, drinking and fathering a pack of 13 children. The song is reputed to have been composed by fellow huntsman, John Woodcock Graves, during a convivial session in a Caldbeck Inn. His gravestone is embellished with a faithful hound, hunting horns and strings of hops; the essential ingredient of his favourite brew. Were he alive today, he would no doubt delight at the resurgence of small craft breweries across his old hunting grounds.

Priest's Mill

*Parked up at The
Lakes Distillery
in Setmurthy*

From Caldbeck, head west on the **B5299** towards
Uldale. Follow this road through Whelpo, up and over
Aughertree Fell and down into **Uldale**. Binsey, the fell we
met earlier in the ride, confronts you as you leave the
village. After 6km, cross the A591 at a staggered junction and follow the B5291 through the flat fields at the
northern end of **Bassenthwaite Lake** and across **River
Derwent**. Ignore signs for Cockermouth at Setmurthy
and stick with this road towards Higham Hall, eventually
forking right into a lane that runs along the south side of
Setmurthy Common and back into Cockermouth. ▶

Based in a renovated
1850s' model farm at
Setmurthy, the Lakes
Distillery produces
whisky, gin and
vodka and makes an
excellent cake stop
before the final run
into Cockermouth.

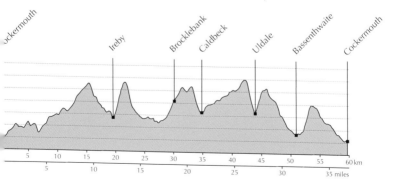

THE SOUTH WEST

ROUTE 10
Back o' Sellafield and Wasdale Head

Distance	64km (40 miles)
Climb	622m
Grade	Medium/moderate
Time	4–5hrs
OS maps	89, 96
Cafés/pubs	Eskdale Green, Ravenglass, Drigg, Beckermet, Calder Bridge, Wasdale Head, Nether Wasdale, Santon Bridge
Start and finish	Eskdale Green (NY142 001)
Maximum gradient	10%

A ride of extremes that goes through historic Ravenglass, then follows a cycle path between the shore and Sellafield before heading inland to visit Wasdale on the way home. Today the Sellafield complex reprocesses nuclear material including that from the original nuclear reactors at Windscale and Calder Hall, which are currently being decommissioned. The site is said to house the two most hazardous industrial buildings in Western Europe; a fact that will no doubt stick with you as you skirt the perimeter fence.

Leave Eskdale Green heading south towards Ulpha. Just before Birker Fell, turn right towards Birkby Road following the River Esk down the valley to meet the **A595**. Turn right towards Workington and climb up and over the southern slopes of Muncaster Fell and past Muncaster Castle. Turn left into **Ravenglass**, then just alongside the railway, turn right to follow National Cycle Route 72 over the River Mite to Saltcoats. Follow this road to the junction with the A595 and turn left towards Workington still following the NCR72 into **Holmrook**.

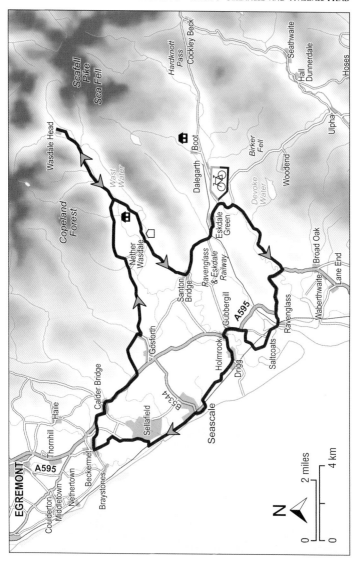

Those with skinny tyres might want to carry their bike for short distances on the track behind Sellafield as there are sections of cinder, plastic lattice and drifting sand.

Just after crossing the River Irt, in the centre of the village, turn left and ride through **Drigg** to **Seascale**. As the road turns inland under the railway, turn left on to NCR72 and enjoy some traffic free cycling for a while. The cycle path goes all the way to Sellafield Station with the nuclear site to your right and the Irish Sea to your left before rejoining the road near the isolated St Bridget's Church on the outskirts of **Beckermet**. ◄ Turn right through this attractive village and out the other side to meet the A595. Turn right towards Barrow and cycle through **Calder Bridge**. Turn left at Boonwood Garden Centre into an unmarked road that leads uphill before turning right and dropping sharply down into Wellington. This village is a satellite of Gosforth Bridge, but unless you need supplies, turn left at the T junction and climb steeply out of the valley towards **Nether Wasdale** and Wastwater Head.

This road starts out as pastoral with easy pedalling beneath a canopy of trees, and then gets increasingly dramatic with views of Wasdale Screes plunging 600m and more from the summit of Illgill Head all the way into the murky depths below.

Ignore the turning to Nether Wasdale and continue to Wasdale Head with the impressive panorama of Yewbarrow, Kirkfell, Great Gable and Scafell Pike as a

Muted tones in Seascale

backdrop to the neatly walled fields that were first enclosed by Vikings. It's a good place to stretch the legs, perhaps with a visit to St Olaf's Church. Surrounded by yew trees in the middle of the fields, it is reputed to be the smallest church in England and contains the graves of many climbers who came to grief on the surrounding crags.

Wasdale Head Inn framed by the old yew trees that surround St Olaf's church

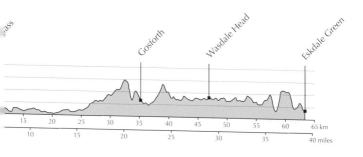

WASDALE: HOME OF THE KING OF FELL RUNNERS

The Bob Graham Round is the fell-running equivalent of the Fred Whitton Challenge with runners traversing 42 or more fell tops with a height of at least 2000ft within 24 hours of starting out from the Moot Hall in Keswick. The round covers approximately 106km (66 miles) of ground with 8200m of ascent. It was first done in 1932 by Bob Graham (1889–1966), a Keswick guest house owner, and since then nearly 2000 individuals have successfully completed the feat with the fastest time of 13 hours, 53 minutes being held by Bobby Bland of the famous Kendal fell-running dynasty since 1982.

Now over 80, locally born Joss Naylor is recognised as the greatest fell runner of them all. His achievements include running 72 summits in 24 hours, completing all summits in Wainwright's Lakeland guidebooks within seven days at the age of 50 and running 70 fell tops in less than 21 hours at the age of 70. Awesome, when you remember that going downhill is hardly freewheeling.

Looking north along Wast Water

When it's time to go, ride back down the valley sticking close to Wast Water all the way, turn left at the T junction at the bottom and ride up through the woodlands to **Santon Bridge**. Then turn left again at the junction in the village and follow signs for **Eskdale**.

ROUTE 11

The Far South West from Ravenglass

Distance	56km (35 miles)
Climb	1087m
Grade	Medium/hard
Time	5–6hrs
OS maps	96
Cafés/pubs	Ravenglass, Seathwaite, Boot, Eskdale Green
Start and finish	Car park on main A595 in Ravenglass (SD 096 967)
Maximum gradient	30%
Major climbs	Corney Fell: 6.7km, 361m, 19%; Hardknott Pass: 2.1km, 180m, 30%.

This is a gem of a ride in the far south west of the national park that climbs to a height of 402m over Corney Fell giving memorable views out over the Irish Sea, which is a mere 7km away. Then after some easier pedalling up the Duddon Valley, it's time for the daddy of them all – Hardknott Pass from the east.

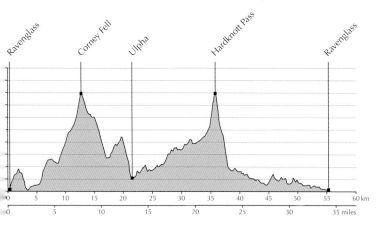

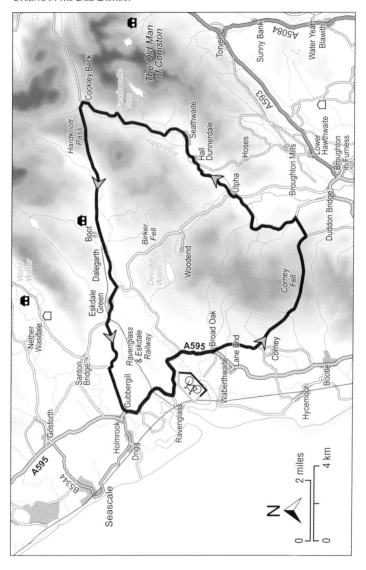

*Starting out up
the normally quiet
Corney Fell, which
can be periodically
busy with commuter
traffic from the
nearby Sellafield
reprocessing site.*

Turn left out of the car park and follow the A595 below
Muncaster Castle and over the River Esk. It is a busy
main road and unless there are any pedestrians about it
makes sense to take to the pavement. After a couple of
miles, turn left on an oblique bend, following signs for
Corney and Broughton. This minor road climbs pleasantly all the way up **Corney Fell** with a brief kick over
Buckbarrow Beck and another just past Kinmont Beck
before crossing the saddle at the summit at a height of
402m above sea level.

After 3km of fast descending down Thwaites Fell,
bear left following a sign for Broughton and soon afterwards turn left again to follow a sign for Whitehaven.
This single track lane is called Bobbin Mill Hill. ▶ After a
bend, the road drops steeply down to **Ulpha** on the banks
of the River Duddon through a broad valley of grassy

The lane is named
after the craft of
bobbin making,
which was carried
out in the area using
wood from the
many copses and
water from the fast
flowing becks to
power the lathes.

A rider struggles up Hardknott Pass as we descend into Eskdale

fields neatly stitched with dry stone walls and tidy thorn hedges. Anyone who does most of their cycling in an urban environment will think it paradise.

The route sticks close to the river all the way up the valley through **Dunnerdale** where it switches across to the other bank and onwards through Seathwaite where The Newfield Inn may prove to be too tempting to pass. It is easy riding, but once at **Cockley Beck**, paradise is over for a while as the route swings westwards to climb **Hardknott Pass**. The first kilometre is just a warm up for the climbing to come and when it comes, it comes with a vengeance. On the Landranger Series of maps, the Ordnance Survey manages to cram seven chevrons into half a kilometre making it impossible to tell if they are single chevrons representing a gradient of 14–20 per cent or double chevrons representing a gradient above 20 per cent. In fact, it should not be called Hardknott Pass at all because hard it most definitely is, averaging a gradient of 17 per cent for the next 500 metres. Even the road wavers, seemingly unsure as to whether it too will make it to the summit. But it does, and so too will you tipping over the summit at a height 393m which is only 9m less than Corney Fell earlier in the ride.

With the hard work done for the day, it's time to enjoy the descent taking care to keep your speed under control in order to navigate the hairpin bends. Once down in the valley, it's easy rolling through **Boot** and **Eskdale Green** with pubs galore. First The Woolpack with its own Harter Gold lager named after the fell across the road. Further down the valley come Brook House Inn and the Boot Inn, both with a changing range of craft beers. Then at the end of the valley is the King George IV Inn, again stocking beers that the notorious bon viveur that gives the pub its name might have enjoyed. ▶

Fans of real ales could idle away many happy hours riding around the lower reaches of the Eskdale Valley.

Stop to take a souvenir photograph at the road sign warning of 30 per cent gradients and then turn right at the T junction in front of the King George IV Inn towards Ravenglass. After the Bower House Inn, turn left towards Holmrook and left again at the next T junction still in the direction of Holmrook. After 3km, turn left on to the A595 and follow the road through **Ravenglass**, home of the famous Ravenglass and Eskdale Steam Railway, and back to the start.

Easy riding out towards the Cumbria coast

Heading along the A595 below Muncaster Castle

RAVENGLASS

Ravenglass is unique as the only coastal town within the boundaries of the Lake District National Park. Being at the confluence of three rivers: the Esk, Mite and Irt, makes access to the harbour difficult at low water, but that did not deter the Romans from establishing an important naval base here in the second century to supply their outposts in North West Britain along a network of roads such as Hardknott Pass and High Street that radiate out across the district. They stayed for 300 years, but today there is little evidence of their presence other than a bath house, which is one of the largest remaining Roman structures in England covering an area of 27 metres by 12 metres and with walls up to 3.6m high.

It is thought that nearby Muncaster Castle is built on the foundations of a Roman fort that was associated with the main Roman site of Glannoventa at Ravenglass; the place name Muncaster containing the Latin word castra meaning encampment or fort. However, the Romans only stayed for 300 years whereas the Pennington family have lived at Muncaster Castle for 800 years, ever since King John granted the estate to Alan de Penitone in 1208.

ROUTE 12

Around the Furness Fells from Broughton

Distance	46km (29 miles)
Climb	1024m
Grade	Short/challenging
Time	4–5hrs
OS maps	96
Cafés/pubs	Broughton in Furness, Grizebeck, Broughton Mills
Start and finish	Broughton in Furness (SD 212 375)
Maximum gradient	15%
Major climbs	Bank House Moor: 1.8km, 200m, 14%

It is easy to be envious of the cycling clubs from the towns of south and west Cumbria as they have access to a variety of terrain for their club rides. This ride takes in the fells on either side of Broughton-in-Furness giving fine views out over Duddon Sands to the Isle of Man and beyond.

Head east out of Broughton in Furness following the road that runs alongside the Manor Arms to meet the A595. Turn left towards Grizebeck and climb up and around Bank End, before turning right into a steep lane that drops down to join the A595 road. At the T junction at the bottom, turn right towards Barrow. Then after a kilometre, turn left through the small hamlet of Chapels and climb up a narrow lane. ▶ At **Beck Side**, turn left towards Ulverston and steadily climb to the summit of Bank House Moor encountering occasional stretches with gradients above 15 per cent. On a clear day, the views over the sands of the Duddon Estuary make it all worthwhile. Burlington Slate Quarry above Chapels is said to be the largest man-made hole in Europe, but little is visible from below as access is by tunnels through the hillside.

Just over the top turn left towards Lowick, traversing the moor, then turning right and left at a staggered

This lane is known as the Lady Moyra Incline after a tramway named in honour of Lady Moyra Cavendish (1871–1946), whose family still quarries slate in the hills above Chapels.

Taking a break to look back across the Duddon Sands on the climb up Bank House Moor

junction with the **B5281**. To the south east, you can see the nuclear power station at Heysham on the far side of Morecambe Bay. Further on, cross the A5092 heading towards Coniston, then turn left into an unmarked lane on the outskirts of **Lowick** and shortly afterwards left again at a fork in the road. At the next T junction, turn right up and over the shoulder of Blawith Knott passing

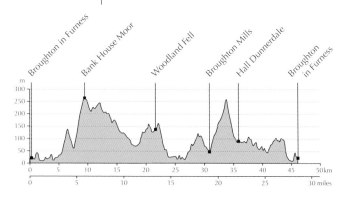

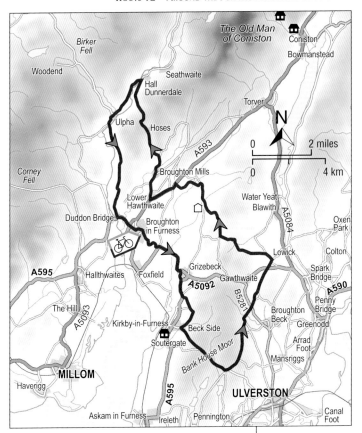

through a couple of farm gates along the way. Turn right at the next junction too, still heading for Coniston. Turn left at the first sign for Broughton, passing through the tiny hamlet of Rosthwaite before a short, sharp climb up and over the old railway line to meet the A593. Turn left on to the main road towards Broughton and follow it to **Lower Hawthwaite**, where a turn on the right leads down to **Broughton Mills**. There is a steady climb up through

Approaching Hoses after climbing the Dunnerdale Fells

Hoses and over the coll between the Dunnerdale Fells with the reward of an enjoyable descent down to meet the River Duddon. Turn left down the Duddon Valley and ride through **Ulpha** all the way to the junction with the A595 at **Duddon Bridge**. Turn left and ride back to the start at **Broughton**.

DUDDON FURNACE

If you cross Duddon Bridge and turn immediately right towards Corney you soon come to Duddon Furnace. It is difficult to think of this wooded valley as being industrial, but once it had everything necessary to produce iron. The iron ore (haematite) was mined locally from the Middle Ages onwards and smelted in primitive hearths or 'bloomeries' that were located in places with an ample supply of timber for making charcoal and water power for driving the bellows that pumped air into the combustion chamber. Good access to the sea was also important for both bringing in barges of ore and for taking away the pig iron that would eventually be made into anchors, chains and other iron work for ships.

There were other furnaces in the area, but Duddon Furnace is the most complete example that survives and one of the most impressive

The restored remains of Duddon Iron Works

charcoal-fired blast furnaces in Britain. The furnace was originally established in 1736 as a joint venture between the Cunsey Company and the Backbarrow Company that had furnaces nearby. However this was hardly a local business. In 1737, the partners of the Cunsey Company included Edward Hall of Cranage, Cheshire; Warine Falkner of Rugeley, Staffordshire; Thomas Cotton of Eardley, Cheshire and Edward Kendall of Stourbridge, Worcestershire. All of these men were from families that played a leading role in the development of the iron industry in the 18th century, setting up numerous furnaces throughout Great Britain.

Members of the Kendall family were among the first to move away from using charcoal as a source of carbon. In 1779, they built the first in a series of coke-fuelled furnaces at Ebbw Vale in South Wales as coke was both more efficient and cheaper than charcoal. Replacing water power with steam engines in the first part of the 19th century resulted in further improvements in scale and productivity marking the beginning of a long decline in charcoal-fired smelting.

After Duddon Ironworks closed in 1866, the site became derelict. It has now been partially restored, and is in the care of the Lake District National Park. An information panel gives a description of the various parts of the furnace.

THE SOUTH EAST

ROUTE 13
Around Grizedale Forest

Distance	32km (20 miles)
Climb	654m
Grade	Short/moderate
Time	2–3hrs
OS maps	90, 96
Cafés/pubs	Ambleside, Barngates, Oxen Park, Satterthwaite, Grizedale, Hawkshead, Outgate
Start and finish	Grizedale Forest Visitor Centre (SD 336 944)
Maximum gradient	12%

Other than 500 metres of hard climbing up Bessy Banks Lane, this is a fairly relaxing ride with plenty of attractions along the way, especially so if you are interested in literature with connections to John Ruskin at Brantwood, Arthur Ransome at Rusland and Beatrix Potter at Hawkshead.

GRIZEDALE

There have been three Grizedale Halls: the first dating from the 17th century and the last from 1905, when Harold Brocklebank built a neo Gothic mansion. In late 18th century, the Brocklebank family ran a successful shipbuilding business at Whitehaven, but moved to Liverpool in 1819. Despite set backs during the Napoleonic Wars, they managed to grow their business during the 19th century until it was acquired by the Cunard shipping company in 1911 with Harold and other family members becoming directors.

After his death in 1936, the hall and 4500 acres of woodland that make up the Grizedale estate became the property of the Forestry Commission. The hall was used as a prisoner of war camp in World War II before being systematically dismantled in the 1950s leaving only a small part of the hall and the terraced garden.

Today, Grizedale is a popular tourist destination with a sculpture trail, mountain biking tracks, an aerial assault course and a visitor centre with a bike shop, café and shop.

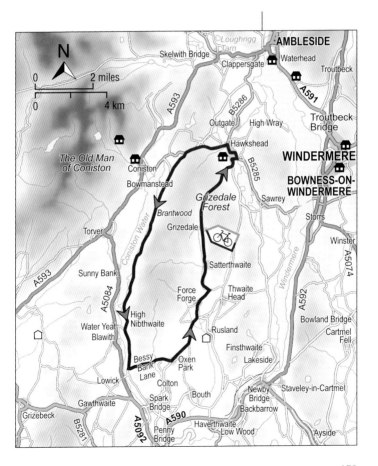

Easy riding below a canopy of new leaves on the eastern shore of Coniston Water

Villagers would pay their rents and answer for their crimes at Hawkshead Courthouse, which is all that remains of a 15th-century manorial farm belonging to Furness Abbey.

Leave Grizedale and head north towards Hawkshead with some gentle climbing before a steep descent down through Roger Ground to meet the main road along the west side of Elterwater. Turn left to reach **Hawkshead** then left around the eastern side of the village following the B5285 and signs for Ambleside. Turn left at the junction near Hawkshead Courthouse, still following the B5285 towards Coniston. ◄

Once over to top of Hawkshead Hill, there is a turning on the left that leads to the east of Lake.

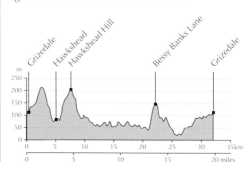

180

Stop for a minute here and marvel at the design of the **water trough**, which has a seat and drinking fountain for the weary traveller, a trough for their horse and a bowl for their dog. Now a Grade II listed building, it was erected in 1885 by Susanna Beever, who became a close friend of the polymath John Ruskin in her later life and is buried next to him in the churchyard in Coniston.

At the bottom of this lane, turn left towards Newby Bridge and cycle past Brantwood, Ruskin's home from 1872 until his death in 1900, and along the length of **Coniston Water** until its outflow into the River Crake. At the southern end of the lake, look out for one of Anthony Gormley's iconic statues silently staring back toward the Central Fells. Just after High Nibthwaite, turn left towards Oxen Park up Bessy Bank Lane. After the easy rolling alongside Coniston Water, climbing up this prettily named lane comes as a shock to the system with a 500 metre stretch of road with an average gradient in excess of 10 per cent. Once clear of the trees, there is a good view of Dow Crag and The Old Man of Coniston across the lake. Keep left in Bandrake Head, following signs for Satterthwaite, and ride to **Oxen Park**. Turn left in the centre of the village towards Grizedale and ride through Satterthwaite to **Grizedale**. ▶

Just off route at Rusland is the grave of the author Arthur Ransome who used many Lakeland locations in his *Swallows and Amazons* series of children's books.

One of Anthony Gormley's iconic statues in High Nibthwaite

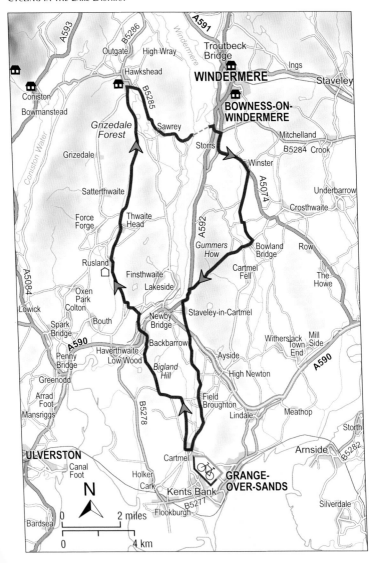

ROUTE 14

Across Windermere from Cartmel

Distance	54km (34 miles)
Climb	881m
Grade	Medium/moderate
Time	4–5hrs
OS maps	97
Cafés/pubs	Cartmel, Backbarrow, Hawkshead, Far Sawrey, Near Sawrey, Bowness-on-Windermere, Winster, Bowland Bridge, Strawberry Bank
Start and finish	Cartmel (SD 378 788)
Maximum gradient	12%

You might choose this ride because it passes right through the heart of Beatrix Potter country and past a host of other tourist attractions giving plenty of reasons for frequent stops. Or you might choose it just for the enjoyment of riding the miles of quiet lanes that run through this heavily wooded part of the Lake District.

Park at the public parking on the racecourse and ride up the road on its eastern side away from Cartmel. Turn right into Greenbank Lane and ride to Wood Broughton following National Cycle Route 20. At the T junction at the end, turn left still following NCR20, then right at the next T junction heading towards Haverthwaite. Turn right opposite the second entrance to Bigland Hall, abandoning the NCR20 and drop down through the hillside hamlets of High Brow Edge then Low Brow Edge to meet the A590 at **Backbarrow**. Dismount and cross the main road using the pedestrian reservation, then turn quickly left into the lower part of the village, which is dominated by a luxury hotel based in a factory that once produced 'Dolly Blue', an essential laundry whitener before domestic washing machines. Turn right immediately after crossing

The Beatrix Potter museum in Hawkshead is housed in a building that was once the legal offices of her husband William Hellis

the River Leven, then turn left after passing under the Lakeside and Haverthwaite Railway.

At the top of this lane, turn left, then quickly right and ride to the end where the only sign points to Haverthwaite. Ignore that and turn right. There are no

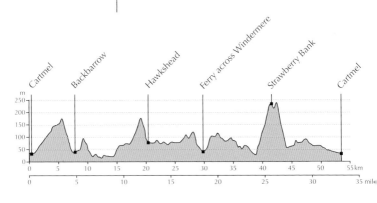

184

more junctions for another 10km, so enjoy the woodlands and gentle brooks all the way to Esthwaite Water. Turn left at the T Junction at the end of the road and ride into **Hawkshead**, which is a good place to break for coffee or lunch. Now head south towards Windermere following the B5285 and cycle through Near Sawrey and Far Sawrey to reach the ferry.

> Hill Top, the small 17th-century farmhouse in Near Sawrey, which Beatrix Potter purchased in 1905 with the proceeds of her first book, is open for most of the year. However, as it is a small house, there is a timed-ticket system in operation and visitors may sometimes have to wait.

There has been a crossing here for over 500 years. The original craft were rowed, then driven by steam and the current ones have diesel engines. They carry 100

Looking north up Esthwaite Water towards Hawkshead

Just off the route is Blackwell, a magnificent arts and crafts house of 1901 built by MH Baillie Scott containing furniture, ceramics and fabrics by the leading designers of the time.

passengers and operate every 20 minutes throughout the day with the exception of Christmas Day and Boxing Day. The current fare is £1.00 for a cyclist and their bike. Coming from peaceful woods in Grizedale into the bustle of **Bowness-on-Windermere** can be either a shock or a pleasant change depending on your point of view.

Head up away from the lake and turn right to follow the A5074 towards Lancaster. Turn left at the next junction and climb Longtail Hill to meet the main A5074 at the top. Turn right still heading for Lancaster and ride to Winster. ◄

Turn right opposite the Brown Horse Inn in **Winster** and follow this narrow lane all the way to Bowland Bridge using the ample signposts as guidance along the way. Turn right at the T junction at the end of this road and ride through **Bowland Bridge** and up Strawberry Bank. This is a sweet name for such a vicious little hill with an average gradient of 11 per cent, but it is soon over. There is further climbing to come at Fell Foot Brow, but it is far gentler and has the reward of fine views down on to Windermere and more than 2km of descent through the plantations of Fell Foot Park. Turn left at the junction with the A592, and then left again to **Staveley-in-Cartmel**. Cross the A590 towards Cartmel and follow this road all the way back to the start.

CARTMEL

Cartmel retains much of its medieval origins with the 12th-century Cartmel Priory, a traditional market square where the villagers once traded and a web of narrow lanes. Right next to the village is Cartmel Racecourse, which is thought to have its origins in mule races organised by the monks for their own entertainment in the middle of the fifteenth century. Flat racing and steeple chasing started here in 1856 possibly by the Cavendish family of nearby Holker Hall who today manage the racecourse as part of the estate. A busy calendar of racing brings many visitors to Cartmel, which prospers as a centre for good food including locally made cheeses, breads, craft beers and sticky toffee pudding. The village is also home to the award-winning L'Enclume, which was voted the UK's Top Restaurant by the *Good Food Guide* in 2014. It describes itself as 'relaxed', although I doubt whether that extends to sweaty Lycra.

ROUTE 15
A circuit around Whitbarrow

Distance	46km (29 miles)
Climb	504m
Grade	Short/hard
Time	3–4hrs
OS maps	97
Cafés/pubs	Grange-over-Sands, Longhowe End, Gilpin Bridge, Brigsteer, Underbarrow, Witherslack, High Newton, Cartmel
Start and finish	Grange-over-Sands (SD 412 712)
Maximum gradient	20%

This circuit around Whitbarrow is a bit like the damsons that grow in the area – sweet but with a sting in the tail. The first half heads northwards up the flat easy-rolling expanses of the Lyth Valley then turns south along the Winster Valley with a short, but sharp, kick over Newton Fell before returning through Cartmel to Grange-over-Sands.

Looking across the Kent Estuary to Grange-over-Sands at twilight

GRANGE-OVER-SANDS – THE RESORT WITH NOWHERE TO SWIM

The opening of the Ulverston and Lancaster Railway in 1857 turned a small fishing village on the north side of Morecambe Bay into a popular seaside resort; the 'over-Sands' suffix being adopted around 1900 at the insistence of the local vicar who was fed up with his post going to Grange in Borrowdale.

The River Kent used to flow right along the town's mile-long promenade but over the years its course migrated south leaving just sand and mud. To keep the tourists coming, an open air Art Deco lido was built in 1932 and this ran until 1993. A new swimming pool called Berners Swimming Pool was opened with great fanfare in 2003, but closed in 2006 after structural faults resulted in financial difficulties. The Berners Pool was demolished in 2013 and the land put up for sale to raise funds for restoring the lido, which was designated a Grade II heritage asset in 2011. A growing enthusiasm for open-air swimming should ensure its success, especially given the town's favourable microclimate.

Meanwhile, a sustained period of strong easterly winds in 2007 has caused the course of the River Kent to start to move northwards. So perhaps the town may eventually be re-named Grange-on-Sea.

John 'Iron-Mad' Wilkinson (1728–1808), the Workington-born iron founder lived at Castle Head on the knoll across the golf course – and true to form, he was buried in an iron coffin.

Head east along Main Street past the park and bear right at the mini-roundabout following the B5277 towards Lindale. After a few hundred yards, turn right on to Meathorp Road towards the golf club. ◀

Once across the River Winster, the railway turns away over the Kent Estuary but the road swings northwards through **Meathop**. Sea air and spring water were once believed to benefit tuberculosis sufferers and in 1891 one of the first sanatoriums in the country was established at Meathop. Follow the blue cycle way-mark at the V junction in the middle of the village and turn left once out of the village, along the route of the Cumbria Coastal Way. Were it not for the rounded hills to the north, one could easily believe this was fenland, and in many ways it is, having been built up from alluvial soils deposited along the banks of the estuary.

On reaching the busy **A590**, follow the cycle path sign to the right and take the subway under the dual carriageway. Keep following the cycle route, turning right at The Derby Arms and going straight on for the next 3km before bearing left across a footbridge to follow a purpose built stretch of cycle path along to the pub at Gilpin Bridge. Loop around behind the pub ignoring the first junction and turn left alongside the garage still following the blue cycle route signs. After 500 metres, turn left by a clump of trees and follow this unmarked road to

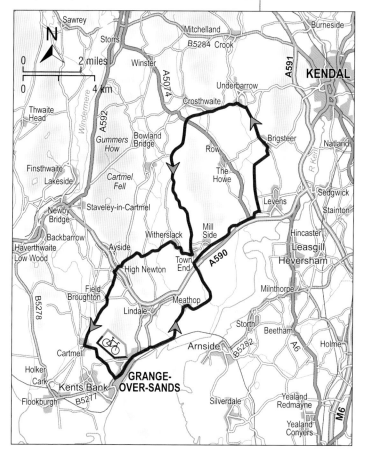

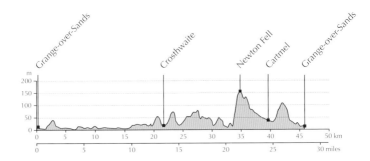

The lime-rich soils of the sheltered Lyth Valley are ideal for growing damsons and the orchards are white with blossom in spring making a memorable ride.

Brigsteer nestling in the trees on the escarpment. Turn left at the T junction at the end of the village and follow the road to Underbarrow. ◄

Turn left in the centre of **Underbarrow** towards Crosthwaite, left again just before the village towards Lyth and then immediately right down an unmarked lane. Cross the A5074 heading towards Cartmel. The road climbs steadily through the wooded western flanks of Whitbarrow to **Witherslack**. Turn right towards Newton

Whitbarrow – a distinctive limestone hill on the southern boundary of the Lake District National Park – seen from across the River Kent

in the upper part of the village and then left in the lower part, still heading for Newton. This road crosses the River Winster and the road down the western edge of the valley then climbs up Newton Fell with gradients of up to 20 per cent. Turn left at the T junction at the top and drop down into **High Newton**, going straight across the first set of crossroads and left at the next T junction, crossing the A590 by a bridge. Turn left and then right following signs for Cartmel and follow this road for 5km all the way to **Cartmel**. ▶ At the triangular green follow the sign to Grange, climbing up and over the southern tip of Hampsfell before dropping down into the town. Turn left on meeting the B5277 to return to the start.

Parked up outside Cartmel Priory

The priory and the village centre are to the right and are both well worth visiting.

APPENDIX A
Useful contacts

Tourist information centres

Bowness-On-Windermere
Lake District National Park TIC
Glebe Rd
Bowness-on-Windermere
Cumbria LA23 3HJ
Tel 0845 901 0845
www.lakedistrict.gov.uk

Keswick
Lake District National Park TIC
Moot Hall
Keswick
Cumbria CA12 5JR
Tel 0845 901 0845
www.lakedistrict.gov.uk

Ullswater
Lake District National Park TIC
Beckside car park
Glenridding
Penrith
Cumbria CA11 0PD
Tel 017684 82414
www.lakedistrict.gov.uk

Cycle shops and cycle hire
The following is a list of cycle shops and
places where cycles can be hired (H).

Ambleside
Biketreks (H)
Rydal Rd
Ambleside
Cumbria LA22 9AN
Tel 015394 31245
www.bike-treks.co.uk

Ghyllside Cycles (H)
The Slack
Ambleside
Cumbria LA22 9DQ
Tel 015394 33592
www.ghyllside.co.uk

Cockermouth
4 Play Cycles
25–31 Market Place
Cockermouth
Cumbria CA13 9NH
Tel 01900 823377

Grizedale
Grizedale Mountain Bikes (H)
Grizedale Centre
Grizedale
Ambleside
Cumbria LA22 0QJ
Tel 01229 860335

Kendal
Askew Cycles
The Old Brewery
Wildman St
Kendal
Cumbria LA9 6EN
Tel 01539 728057

Brucies Bike Shop
9 Kirkland
Kendal
Cumbria LA9 5AF
Tel 01539 727230

Evans Cycles
113 Stricklandgate
Kendal
Cumbria LA9 4RF
Tel 01539 740087
www.evanscycles.com

Keswick
Keswick Bikes (H)
133 Main St
Keswick
Cumbria CA12 5NJ
Tel 017687 73355
www.keswickbikes.co.uk

Keswick Mountain Bikes (H)
18 Otley Rd
Keswick
Cumbria CA12 5LE
Tel 017687 80586
www.keswickbikes.co.uk

Lakeland Pedlar Bicycle Centre
Hendersons Yard
Keswick
Cumbria CA12 5JD
Tel 017687 75752
www.keswickbikes.co.uk

Cyclewise
Whinlatter Forest
Braithwaite
Keswick
Cumbria CA12 5TW
Tel 017687 78711
www.cyclewise.co.uk

Penrith
Arragons Cycle Centre
2 Brunswick Rd
Penrith
Cumbria CA11 7LU
Tel 01768 890344
www.arragons.com

Harper Cycles
1–2 Middlegate
Penrith
Cumbria CA11 7PG
Tel 01768 864475

Shap
Cycles Shap
1 Cross Garth
Shap
Penrith
Cumbria CA10 3NN
Tel 07473 808248

Staveley
Wheelbase Lakeland Ltd (H)
Staveley Mill Yard
Back Lane
Staveley, Kendal
Cumbria LA8 9LR
Tel 01539 821443
www.wheelbase.co.uk

Ulverston
DC Cycles Ltd
5 Union Place
Ulverston
Cumbria LA12 7HS
Tel 01229 440417
www.dc-cycles.co.uk

Gill Cycles
Unit 10
Lightburn Trading Estate
Ulverston
Tel 01229 581116
www.gillcycles.co.uk

APPENDIX B
Accommodation

Hostels and camping barns

Simple hostels and camping barns marked (S) in the list below generally do not provide bed linen, rarely provide cooking facilities and occasionally do not have electricity. Check the facilities before booking to avoid surprises.

Ambleside
Ambleside Backpackers
Iveing Cottage
Old Lake Rd
Ambleside
Cumbria LA22 0DJ
Tel 015394 32340
www.amblesidehostel.co.uk

YHA Ambleside
Waterhead
Ambleside
Cumbria LA22 0EU
Tel 0845 371 9620
www.yha.org.uk

Arnside
Arnside Independent Hostel
Oakfield Lodge
Redhills Rd
Arnside
Cumbria LA5 0AT
Tel 01524 761781
www.arnsideindependenthostel.co.uk

Borrowdale
Derwentwater Independent Hostel
Barrow House
Borrowdale
Keswick
Cumbria CA12 5UR

Tel 017687 77246
www.derwentwater.org

Dinah Hoggus Camping Barn (S)
Stonecroft
Borrowdale
Keswick
Cumbria CA12 5XB
Tel 017687 77689
www.lakelandcampingbarns.co.uk

YHA Borrowdale
Longthwaite
Borrowdale
Keswick
Cumbria CA12 5XE
Tel 0845 371 9624
www.yha.org.uk

Broughton In Furness
Fell End Camping Barn (S)
Thornthwaite
Woodland Hall
Broughton in Furness
Cumbria LA20 6DF
Tel 01229 716340
www.lakelandcampingbarns.co.uk

Buttermere
Cragg Camping Barn (S)
Cragg Farm
Buttermere
Cockermouth
Cumbria CA13 9XA
Tel 017687 70204
www.lakelandcampingbarns.co.uk

YHA Buttermere
Buttermere
Cockermouth
Cumbria CA13 9XA
Tel 0845 371 9508
www.yha.org.uk

Cockermouth
YHA Cockermouth
Double Mills
Cockermouth
Cumbria CA13 0DS
Tel 0845 371 9313
www.yha.org.uk

Coniston
YHA Coniston Copper Mines
Coniston
Cumbria LA21 8HP
Tel 0845 371 9630
www.yha.org.uk

Those riding on skinny tyres
should note that this hostel is
1 mile up a rough track.

YHA Coniston Holly Howe
Far End
Coniston
Cumbria LA21 8DD
Tel 0845 371 9511
www.yha.org.uk

Elterwater
Elterwater Hostel
Elterwater
Ambleside LA22 9HX
Tel 015394 37245
www.elterwaterhostel.co.uk

Ennerdale
YHA Ennerdale
Cat Crag
Ennerdale
Cleator
Cumbria CA23 3AX
Tel 0845 371 9116
www.yha.org.uk

Those riding on skinny tyres
should note that this hostel is
2 miles up a forest track.

Eskdale
YHA Eskdale
Boot
Holmrook
Cumbria CA19 1TH
Tel 0845 371 9317
www.yha.org.uk

Glenridding
YHA Helvellyn
Greenside
Glenridding
Penrith
Cumbria CA11 0QR
Tel 0845 371 9742
www.yha.org.uk

Those riding on skinny tyres
should note that this hostel is
1 mile up a rough track.

Grasmere
Thorney Howe Hostel
Thorney How
Grasmere
Cumbria LA22 9QW
Tel 01539 435 597
www.thorneyhow.co.uk

YHA Grasmere Butharlyp Howe
Easedale Rd
Grasmere
Cumbria LA22 9QG
Tel 0845 371 9319
www.yha.org.uk

Grizedale
Rookhow Centre
Rusland Valley
Nr Grizedale
Ulverston
Cumbria LA12 8LA
Tel 01229 860231
www.rookhowcentre.co.uk

Hawkshead
YHA Hawkshead
Hawkshead
Ambleside
Cumbria LA22 0QD
Tel 0845 371 9321
www.yha.org.uk

Hesket Newmarket
Hudscales Camping Barn (S)
Hudscales Farm
Hesket Newmarket
Wigton
Cumbria CA7 8JZ
Tel 016974 78637
www.lakelandcampingbarns.co.uk

Honister
YHA Honister Pass
Seatoller
Keswick
Cumbria CA12 5XN
Tel 0845 371 9522
www.yha.org.uk

Kentmere
Maggs Howe Camping Barn (S)
Maggs Howe
Kentmere
Kendal
Cumbria LA8 9JP
Tel 01539 821689
http://independenthostels.co.uk

Kirkby In Furness
Duddon Sands Hostel
The Ship Inn
Askewgate Brow
Kirkby-in-Furness
Cumbria LA17 7TE
Tel 01229 889454
www.theship1691.co.uk

Langdale
Great Langdale Bunkhouse
Great Langdale
Cumbria LA22 9JU
Tel 01539 437725
www.greatlangdalebunkhouse.co.uk

YHA Langdale
High Close
Loughrigg
Ambleside
Cumbria LA22 9HJ
Tel 0845 371 9748
www.yha.org.uk

Loweswater
Swallow Camping Barn (S)
Waterend Farm
Loweswater
Cockermouth
Cumbria CA13 0SU
Tel 01946 861465
www.lakelandcampingbarns.co.uk

Kendal
Kendal Hostel
118–120 Highgate
Kendal
Cumbria LA9 4HE
Tel 01539 724 006
www.kendalhostel.co.uk

Wythmoor Farm Camping Barn (S)
Wythmoor Farm
Fiddlergill
Kendal
Cumbria LA8 0DH
Tel 07971018567
www.lakelandcampingbarns.co.uk

Keswick
Denton House Hostel
Penrith Rd
Keswick CA12 4JW
Tel 01768 775351
www.dentonhouse-keswick.co.uk

YHA Keswick
Station Rd
Keswick
Cumbria CA12 5LH
Tel 0845 371 9746
www.yha.org.uk

Newlands
Cat Bells Camping Barn (S)
Low Skelgill
Newlands
Keswick
Cumbria CA12 5UE
Tel 017687 74301
www.lakelandcampingbarns.co.uk

Patterdale
Shepherds Crook Bunkhouse
Noran Bank Farm
Patterdale
Penrith
Cumbria CA11 0NR
Tel 017684 82327

YHA Patterdale
Patterdale
Penrith
Cumbria CA11 0NW
Tel 0845 371 9337
www.yha.org.uk

Penrith
Wayfarers Independent Hostel
19 Brunswick Sq
Penrith
Cumbria CA11 7LR
Tel 01768 866011
www.wayfarershostel.com

Scales
The White Horse Inn
Scales
Nr Threlkeld
Keswick
Cumbria CA12 4SY
Tel 017687 79883
www.thewhitehorse-blencathra.co.uk

Shap
New Ing Lodge
Main St
Shap
Cumbria CA10 3LX
Tel 01933 716719
www.newinglodge.co.uk

St John's In The Vale
St John's in the Vale Camping Barn (S)
Low Bridge End Farm
St John's in the Vale
Keswick
Cumbria CA12 4TS
Tel 017687 79242
www.lakelandcampingbarns.co.uk

Wasdale
Murt Camping Barn (S)
Murt
Wasdale
Cumbria CA20 1ET
Tel 019467 26044
www.lakelandcampingbarns.co.uk

YHA Wastwater
Wasdale Hall
Nether Wasdale
Seascale
Cumbria CA20 1ET
Tel 0845 371 9350
www.yha.org.uk

Windermere
Lake District Backpackers
High St
Windermere LA23 1AF
Tel 015394 46374
www.lakedistrictbackpackers.co.uk

YHA Windermere
Bridge Lane
Troutbeck
Windermere
Cumbria LA23 1LA
Tel 0845 371 9352
www.yha.org.uk

Campsites
The following organisations
have websites that list campsites
in the Lake District.

Camping and Caravanning Club
www.campingandcaravanningclub.co.uk

Cool Camping
www.coolcamping.co.uk

The National Trust
www.nationaltrust.org.uk

Lake District Camping
www.lakedistrictcamping.co.uk

Lake District National Park
www.lakedistrict.gov.uk

UK Campsite
www.ukcampsite.co.uk

Visit England
www.golakes.co.uk

APPENDIX C

What to take

The table below lists optional and essential gear in various categories for summer and winter cycling. It also shows the weight of various bits of kit, and the percentage of your total load that they make up, to help you know where to look for savings to make those Lake District passes just a little easier to tackle.

Riding gear		Off-bike wear	Tools & accessories	Other	Weight
Essential	Optional	Essential	Optional	Essential	
Summer					
Helmet	Waterproof jacket (350gm)	L/s t shirt x 2 (150gm x 2)	Rear light (55gm)	Toiletries (250gm)	
Balaclava or Buff®	Waterproof over-trousers (300gm)	Underwear x 2 (100gm x 2)	Pump (110gm)	Travel towel (135gm)	
Cycling glasses	Overshoes (150gm)	Microfleece top (420gm)	Multi-tool (120gm)	Sun cream (45gm)	
S/s base layer		Travel trousers (450gm)	Spoke key (17gm)	Lip salve (15gm)	
S/s cycling jersey		Socks x 2 (60gm x 2)	Spare inner tube (120gm)	Wet wipes (50gm)	
Arm warmers		Trainers/crocs (600gm)	Self-adhesive patches (20gm)	Compact first aid kit (200gm)	
Cycling gloves		Couple stuff bags (40gm x 2)	Tyre levers (26gm)	Map or GPS & charger (150gm)	
Cycling shorts			Powerlink (5gm)	Guidebook (235gm)	
Leg warmers			Set of cables (50gm)	Itinerary (10gm)	
Socks			Latex gloves (3gm)	Pen (10gm)	
Cycling shoes			Spare bolts x 2 (4gm)	Compact camera (265gm)	
			Cable ties x 2 (3gm)	Phone & charger (270gm)	
				Wallet/cards (100gm)	
Total weight	800gm	2080gm	533gm	2000gm	5413gm
% total	15%	38%	10%	37%	100%

Riding gear	Off-bike wear	Tools & accessories	Other	Weight
Extra for winter				
L/s base layer	Fleece jacket (550gm)	Front light (300gm)		
L/s cycling jersey	Heavier travel trousers (550gm)			
Soft-shell jacket				
Winter cycling gloves				
Bib tights				
Total weight	800gm	3180gm	833gm	2000gm	6813gm
% total	12%	47%	12%	29%	100%

APPENDIX D
Further reading

Cycle Tours In and Around the Lake District, Nick Cotton, Cordee, 2011
Good selection of shorter and less physically demanding rides around the periphery of the Lake District with excellent OS maps.

Cycling in the Lake District,
John Crowe, Skeffington, 1944
Joyous remembrances of adventurous and care-free cycling during the 1940s.

Cycling in the Lake District,
Richard Harries, Moorland, 1984
Masterly documentation of virtually every mile of road in the Lake District that sadly fails to inspire.

Photographing the Lake District,
Stuart Holmes, Fotovue, 2014
Inspirational yet practical guide packed with information about locations and techniques.

A Lake District Miscellany,
Tom Holman, Francis Lincoln, 2007
An entertaining and informative anthology of facts, figures, biographies, recipes, poems and lists.

The Companion Guide to the Lake District, Frank Welsh, Companion Guides, 1989
This is a gem for those who like their travel guides to be informative, witty and opinionated.

A President's Love Affair with the Lake District, Andrew Wilson, Lakeland Press Agency, 1996
An enthusiast's delving into the only famous person who seems to have ridden through the Lake District.

I Never Knew That About the Lake District, Christopher Winn, Ebury Press, 2010
Compendium of interesting facts and stories about the Lake District.

NOTES

Parked up in Chapel Stile looking towards the Langdale Pikes (Stages 5A, B)

DOWNLOAD THE ROUTE
IN GPX FORMAT

All the routes in this guide are available for download from:

www.cicerone.co.uk/778/GPX

as GPX files. You should be able to load them into most formats of mobile device, whether GPS or smartphone.

When you go to this link, you will be asked for your email address and where you purchased the guide, and have the option to subscribe to the Cicerone e-newsletter.

www.cicerone.co.uk

LISTING OF CICERONE GUIDES

For full information on all our
guides, books and eBooks,
visit our website:
www.cicerone.co.uk.

Walking – Trekking – Mountaineering – Climbing – Cycling

Over 40 years, Cicerone have built up an outstanding collection of over 300 guides, inspiring all sorts of amazing adventures.

Every guide comes from extensive exploration and research by our expert authors, all with a passion for their subjects. They are frequently praised, endorsed and used by clubs, instructors and outdoor organisations.

All our titles can now be bought as **e-books**, **ePubs** and **Kindle** files and we also have an online magazine – **Cicerone Extra** – with features to help cyclists, climbers, walkers and trekkers choose their next adventure, at home or abroad.

Our website shows any **new information** we've had in since a book was published. Please do let us know if you find anything has changed, so that we can publish the latest details. On our **website** you'll also find great ideas and lots of detailed information about what's inside every guide and you can buy **individual routes** from many of them online.

It's easy to keep in touch with what's going on at Cicerone by getting our monthly **free e-newsletter**, which is full of offers, competitions, up-to-date information and topical articles. You can subscribe on our home page and also follow us on **Facebook** and **Twitter** or dip into our **blog**.

Cicerone – the very best guides for exploring the world.

CICERONE

2 Police Square Milnthorpe Cumbria LA7 7PY
Tel: 015395 62069 info@cicerone.co.uk
www.cicerone.co.uk and **www.cicerone-extra.com**